CLIP
IN

Praise for *Clip In*

"The authors combine immediately applicable teaching with sound theology to produce healthy, nonmanipulative evangelism. *Clip In* goes beyond common writing on this subject and connects us to the larger mission and purpose of the church. I heartily recommend this marvelous teaching to all my pastors, lay leaders, and congregations."
—Mike Lowry, Resident Bishop, Central Texas Conference, The United Methodist Church

"We all long for our churches to be thriving, compelling, and discipleship-making communities of faith. This book is a helpful and practical resource—a must read for every pastor and congregation seeking to create that type of church."
—Bob Farr, Director of Congregational Excellence, Missouri Annual Conference, The United Methodist Church

"This exceedingly useful book takes into account the changing landscape of church attendance and participation patterns. Readers will learn how to convert good intentions into biblical hospitality through specific plans and practices."
—Lovett H. Weems Jr., Distinguished Professor of Church Leadership and Director of the Lewis Center for Church Leadership of Wesley Theological Seminary

"In this book, Jim and Fiona lead us beyond mere hospitality to loving and welcoming people as a way of life. They show us that hospitality is not the task of a team but must be the culture throughout the organization. They remind me, as a judicatory leader, that our leaders need to feel it in my office too."
—James Bushfield, Director of Connectional Ministry, Indiana Conference, The United Methodist Church

"Some people think that to talk about strategies for loving others is somehow forced or manipulative, like a spiritual, self-serving Dale Carnegie course. Nothing could be further from the truth. Everyone needs empathy training. Jim Ozier's book does a brilliant job of helping people learn how to be more others-focused. After all, isn't this just part two of the summary of all the Law and Prophets, according to Jesus?"
—Len Wilson, author, blogger at lenwilson.us, Creative Director at Peachtree Presbyterian Church

CLIP IN

RISKING HOSPITALITY IN YOUR CHURCH

Jim Ozier & Fiona Haworth

Abingdon Press
Nashville

CLIP IN:
RISKING HOSPITALITY IN YOUR CHURCH

Copyright © 2014 by Abingdon Press

This book is printed on acid-free paper.

Library of Congress Cataloging-in-Publication Data

Ozier, Jim.
    Clip in : risking hospitality in your church / Jim Ozier and Fiona Haworth.
        pages cm
    ISBN 978-1-4267-8892-5 (pbk., adhesive perfect binding : alk. paper) 1. Hospitality—Religious aspects—Christianity. 2. Church greeters. 3. Church marketing. 4. Church growth. I. Title.
    BV4647.H67O95 2014
    253'.7—dc23

                                                    2014020317

Disclaimer: All personal names and identifying details have been changed to protect the identities of persons.

14 15 16 17 18 19 20 21 22 23—10 9 8 7 6 5 4 3 2 1
MANUFACTURED IN THE UNITED STATES OF AMERICA

This book is dedicated to Trietsch Memorial United Methodist Church in Flower Mound, Texas, where most of the ideas and practices in the pages that follow were birthed, tried, tweaked, and implemented.

Contents

"As Easy as Riding a Bike"

Few articles ever used by humanity created so great a revolution in social conditions as the bicycle.

—*U.S. Census Report, 1900*

If you know how to ride a bike, at some point in your life you learned a skill and overcame a fear at the same time. Congratulations! That's what it takes to master the art of hospitality! Oh sure, you also practiced and put effort and energy into riding until it became second nature, and that is what it takes to create a "culture of hospitality."

For many mainline churches there is an uneasy sense that we are pedaling as fast as we can but are still riding uphill, against the wind all the time. It doesn't have to be this way. What makes a bicycle go is the combination of balance and momentum. In the pages that follow, you'll learn how to apply this metaphor to the life of your local church to go farther and faster than you ever imagined!

Worldwide, over a billion people ride bicycles for fun, transportation, or sport. Many of us learned to ride by the age of ten, graduating from the big-wheeled plastic tricycle to training wheels, and then to our first real bike. You can still remember yours, can't you? And most agree that once we learn to ride, we'll probably never forget how. We nod in agreement when someone says, "It's as easy as riding a bike."

Riding a bike is easy, but scientists tell us it is a lot more complex than we realize. A few years ago a scientific team worked for three years to solve the riddle of what keeps a bike from falling over while someone is riding it. Their mathematic formula took lots of calculations and numbers but basically boiled down to this: Inertia forces + gyroscopic forces + the effects of gravity and centrifugal forces = the leaning of the body and the torque applied to the handlebars of a bike. Put more simply, those who do not pedal fast enough to keep moving while keeping the bike straight fall over (Richard Alleyne, "Riding a Bike Is Incredibly Hard, Scientists Discover," *Telegraph* [UK], June 21, 2010).

Back when you were a kid looking down the slope of the gentle hill, or feeling the force of mom or dad pushing the bike (with you on it) to get it going fast enough, you weren't thinking about the science behind riding. You were feeling more than a little bit scared. You were unsure what to do, or how to do it. You were uncertain you could ride at all. How bad would you be hurt, or how embarrassed would you be if you messed up?

But you got through it! Fortunately, the complexity of the science behind riding a bike didn't overwhelm you . . . you weren't even aware of it. Instead, you leveraged the encouragement (or maybe it was the goading and taunting) of friends and family to believe in the simplicity of it. And you rode. You felt the exhilaration of wind blowing in your hair; the rush of confidence; the thrill of trying new things and going new places; the pure joy of pushing the limits and going just a little farther than you had planned.

After you learned to ride, you probably also learned the basics of how to keep riding. Basics like how to tighten the handlebar, adjust the seat, change a flat tire, and put the chain back on the sprocket. Or you quickly found someone who could do it for you! These were the support necessities that made the riding day in and day out possible. In the chapters that follow, you'll learn the equivalent skills that keep a great culture of hospitality going.

Why is it that once we learn to ride a bike, we almost never forget how? There is just something about the skill of riding that intuitively becomes hardwired into us. It becomes second nature. Once we become proficient at balance and momentum, we quickly master the art of leveraging just the right amount of force (pedaling), effort (pulling on the handlebar), direction (steering), and control (braking) to go farther and faster than we ever could have imagined (Ephesians 3:20).

Clipping In

Accomplished cyclists use special biking shoes that actually fasten in to the pedal by way of a mechanical clip. "Clipping in" can be risky because the cyclist's foot is actually locked into place on the pedal, making it dangerous if the bike slows down too much or tips over.

Fortunately, the best "clip in" mechanisms are easy to get in and out of, and, with practice, the cyclist can learn to quickly detach the foot in emergencies.

Riding a bike in this way takes the experience to a different level, ratchets up the risk a notch, and requires greater commitment.

And that's just the point. Clipping in requires the cyclist to commit. First, it requires a monetary investment to purchase and install the right gear. Then, there is an investment of time to learn this new way of riding the bike. Finally, it takes consistent, regular practice over the long haul. Why do serious cyclists do it? As you can guess, the ratcheted-up commitment offers ratcheted-up rewards. When you're clipped in, you are more efficient and more powerful. You can go faster, farther, with less effort. Your momentum is increased, and drag is decreased. The energy you expend results in miles more easily gained. Risk? Yes, clipping in can be risky at first. Commitment? Yes, it requires focus and dedication, a full commitment to change. Reward? Absolutely. Ask any serious cyclist, and they will tell you that clipping in is the only way to ride.

And so it goes for us as we consider hospitality in our churches. We must be willing to take the risk and fully commit, in order to reap the reward.

Creating a Culture of Hospitality

Once a church gets the knack of hospitality, it becomes hardwired into its life . . . and amazing things happen. A culture of hospitality has five key components: (1) intentionality; (2) relationship; (3) interaction; (4) engagement; (5) connection. In the pages that follow you'll learn not only to appreciate and understand each, but also how implementing these components can accelerate your church's growth.

While bicycles have been improved, tricked up, and streamlined over the years, there are basically five components to this timeless machine. For our purposes each corresponds to one of the key components of hospitality:

- Frame—structure that supports everything else (intentionality)

- Wheels—what enable the bike to go (relationship)

- Handlebars—what set direction, plus gyroscopic force for balance (interaction)

- Seat—center of gravity and where the rider sits to engage the bike (engagement)

- Pedals—what produces the forward thrust for momentum (connection)

Riding a bike is a matter of gaining balance and momentum. So is creating a culture of hospitality. Not only do balance and momentum go hand in hand, but they are also dependent upon each other. Perhaps more amazingly, each causes the other. Growing a church requires the same kind of delicate interplay: balancing attention toward existing members and generating momentum by reaching new people. Without both, the church is not likely to grow. Creating a culture of hospitality facilitates each.

There is science and complexity behind riding, but we don't have to be aware of or even understand it to ride. This book will explain some of the complexity behind hospitality: what it is, how to overcome obstacles, how to train, and how to practice. Mainly, however, this book will show how simple hospitality is—how much fun it is simply to get on and ride!

In the country town of Loami, Illinois, where I (Jim) grew up, the best learning-to-ride-a-bike hill was across the street from our house, next to the little Methodist church my family attended. Speeding down that grassy hill, I first overcame the death-defying odds, kept my balance, pedaled, and rode a few hundred feet! Nervously I sat on my new Speed King, the tips of my toes on my outstretched legs barely able to touch the ground, steadying me. My lips quivered. My older brother held the bike, keeping it upright and assuring me: "You can do this. We're gonna run alongside you a few steps to make sure you don't tip over, and then when you get going fast enough, we'll push you on and you'll ride by yourself. It'll be fun!"

No sooner had he spoken than the bike began to move forward. "Take your feet off the ground; put them on the pedals!" Slowly, we accelerated toward the slope. "That's right! There you go! Now pedal faster and keep your hands on the handlebar—steer it straight! Keep your balance!"

My brother stood behind the bike, pushing; my mom stood next to me, steadying. This was quite a sight, I'm sure, as our excited trio cascaded toward the point of no return. Other kids who had already mastered the rite of passage stood by cheering, yelling, laughing. Braver ones started running alongside; some even rode their bikes next to mine, barely at a safe distance.

I don't remember the exact moment, but at some point I felt a distinct push! And the bike I was sitting on took off! It picked up speed. I veered back and forth reflexively for a while as I gained momentum. It worked! I forgot about bruises and scrapes from trying and falling over the last few days. The high of riding was worth the cost of learning! The magic of momentum—riding by myself, getting the feel of it, gaining control, and being able to slow down when I needed or speed up when I wanted—was awesome. My life would never be the same.

It is our hope that this book gives you just the right guidance and push. Your church will never be the same.

I (Fiona) grew up in Scotland, a breathtaking country rich with history and passionately held culture. My parents still live there, neatly tucked under a beautiful range of hills called the Campsies. Growing up, we would hike up into the hills and take in the astonishing view of the Clyde Valley. A road winds up the side of the Campsies, aptly named the Crow Road (as the crow flies). It is ferociously steep and stretches for a good three miles. Through the years, I've watched bold cyclists take the risk on the mighty challenge of the Crow Road! I can't imagine that kind of unrelenting physical exertion, but I do know what is waiting for them at the top of the hill. The risk is worth the reward! It's the most spectacular vision that reaches far beyond anything one could observe at a lower altitude. Utterly exhilarating! Churches willing to take the risk of creating this kind of culture of hospitality see vistas of ministry that they could only imagine before!

So hop on! We think you'll agree that the metaphor of learning to ride a bike, and the lessons we can derive from looking back on that experience, prove to be useful for talking about creating a culture of hospitality in your local church.

The authors acknowledge with gratitude the many colleagues from whom we have learned bits and pieces of great hospitality over the years. Further, we wish to thank Debbie Bushfield, Matt Gaston, Duane VanGiesen, Burt Palmer, Joell Stanislaus, Holly Wright, Jennifer Rader, Liliana Rangel, Gloria Fowler, and the staff at Abingdon Press who read the manuscript in its various iterations, making improvement in both content and presentation.

Introduction

Making First Impressions Last

A bicycle ride around the world begins
with a single pedal stroke.

—*Scott Stoll*

"Do you know what sound the bumblebee makes?"

The question came through a widening smile, his silver hair curled over crusty eyebrows, his left hand holding a small stack of folded worship bulletins. "Do you? Do you know what sound the bee makes?" He pressed, leaning down into her cute face as best an old, wobbly man could.

Dressed up in her Sunday best, the little girl leaned away, uncomprehending, frightened. She shot her parents a pleading look. They were still standing in the church's doorway, equally confused as to who this old gentleman was and what he was doing, not knowing what they should do.

1

Their daughter was a small child and a shy one, not more than five or six. Her dark hair shook as she began to tremble nervously, wanting to run away, groping for her mother's hand.

Too late. His big, bony right hand swirled in exaggerated circular motions spiraling closer and closer to her while he voiced a spirited impression of a bumblebee's *Bzzzzzz*. Then suddenly, with what he considered a playful poke, the spiral climaxed with a sharp pinch above the dress line on her chest! "That old bee will get you, won't he?" he laughed while aiming for yet another sting.

He laughed. No one else did. She sprawled backward, her almond face almost ashen. The old front door greeter lunged to catch her, knocking his glasses off and sending the bulletins into a chaotic spray across the floor. The young, first-time guest shrieked and cried, begging in Spanish for her mother's rescue.

The old gentleman in his tanned suit grinned and said as he haltingly pushed himself up off the floor, "I always get 'em good with that one!"

Needless to say, this episode probably did not leave a good first impression on this young, first-time guest family. This is not a good behavior for greeters or ushers in a church. Especially not toward folks they have never before seen.

It is unlikely this young family would have ever returned anyway because they were Salvadorian Catholics, attending this Protestant church only to honor the baptism of a friend's infant. And the elderly greeter was well-intentioned, doing the same kind of things he had frequently done for years: trying to be fun loving, funny, and engaging.

"How do we train our greeters and ushers to be better at their jobs?" I was asked while on a hospitality consultation and when I heard this tale recounted. The pastors and staff and the hospitality team all seemed to grasp that what had transpired in that episode was so bad it left a lasting impression. Their anguished question came then as no surprise: "How do we do hospitality that is so good it leaves a lasting impression?"

That is what this book is about: creating a first impression that lasts! It is not unlike riding a bike, which requires mastering the art of balance with the necessity of momentum. Creating a culture of hospitality requires balance—balancing the needs of the current congregation with reaching new people; balancing pastoral care of existing folks with evangelistic outreach to new folks; balancing institutional demands with an outward focus. It takes both to keep a church moving forward.

We often teach clergy in workshops this adage: "If you love your people more than stretch them, you will soon become known as their chaplain; if you stretch your people more than you love them, you will soon be known as their former pastor!" Just as in riding a bike, it takes balance to create momentum and momentum to create balance. The two go hand in hand and actually depend upon each other.

So be patient and stay with us, even if you are thinking, "Oh no. The last thing we need is another book on hospitality." Believe me: we've read most every book, listened to every training CD and DVD. We've gone to countless seminars and workshops, and conducted dozens ourselves.

We think you'll find these pages approach hospitality in a unique way. Hopefully at least those readers in the United Methodist tribe will recognize this as follow-up to Bishop Robert Schnase's groundbreaking book *Five Practices of Fruitful Congregations* and to the more recent book *Get Their Name: Grow Your Church by Building New Relationships*, by Bob Farr, Doug Anderson, and Kay Kotan. Our intention here is to put legs and feet on the practices promoted in those books, especially in the area of "radical hospitality."

More than looking for the magic training bullet for hospitality teams to do their *functions* better, this book will teach you how to create a *culture of hospitality* (or as one man quipped after the workshop,

3

"You should call it 'Gospeltality'") practiced regularly and—no pun intended—religiously by *every member every Sunday.*

"Every member every Sunday" can become a characteristic of your church culture. But like learning to ride a bike, you've got to take some risks and try something new or maybe even a bit scary.

This book adopts the definition and characterization of organizational culture from Edgar Schein, Thomas Wren, and others: "Organizational culture develops from shared assumptions of a group that shape their attitudes, actions, and awareness. Simply, it is 'the way we do things around here.' Over time, a certain way of doing things and relating within the group develops, and a culture emerges" (Wren, *The Leader's Companion: Insights on Leadership Through the Ages* [New York: Free Press, 1995]; Schein, *Organizational Culture and Leadership* [San Francisco: Jossey-Bass, 2004]).

Church culture is not so much *what we do* as it is *how we go about doing it.* Every church does hospitality. The question is how your church is hospitable—not simply how you do the programs or functions of hospitality—but the feel, spirit, and style as it is being done.

When it comes to hospitality, we're not just talking about the step-by-step procedures (although you'll learn those) of ensuring a warm, friendly, and engaging experience. Even more important, we are creating a culture of hospitality that is creative, passionate, and relevant—an irresistible one that produces joy, smiles, and fun.

In a church (as in most any other endeavor or organization), making first impressions so good that they last is not the result of people doing things well; it is the result of developing a culture of hospitality. A culture whose DNA runs through every aspect of the church's life; a culture in which hospitality is extended with no response expected. If our hospitality is done with the motive of getting something in return, then it is not biblical, even if we assume that the return is to get people to return.

4

In ancient biblical days, people showered hospitality upon the strangers traveling through barren land because it would give the travelers some respite, and might even save their lives. The host might not ever see the travelers again, but hospitality was extended simply because it was the right thing to do. A culture of hospitality is one that extends graciousness to persons whom we are likely never to see again, just as though they were a top prospect for our church.

The goal of hospitality is not to get people to return. That is its by-product. The goal is to mirror the loving welcome of Jesus Christ and live it out in tangible ways. Hospitality is often associated with being warm, welcoming, and friendly. It includes all that, but if there's nothing more it's like riding a stationary bike: a great exercise that's good for you and feels good but ultimately leaves you spinning your wheels rather than moving forward.

Hospitality that makes a real impact will be built upon intentionality (a strategic process), focus on relationship (personal and genuine), inspire interaction (people taking initiative), create engagement (elicit response) and result in connection (linking people).

A good hospitality response: "Those people sure *seem* friendly."

A great hospitality response: "Those people sure *are* friendly!"

If you stick with us, we will teach you four things:

- First, how to rediscover the forgotten power of introductions: why and how to get church members to introduce themselves to newcomers and to others they don't yet know.

- Second, how to move introductions beyond, "Good to see you," to making connections—the glue to making hospitality stick and those first impressions last.

- Third, how good connections can lead to mastering the emerging phenomenon of recommendation. Why and how to create a culture where attenders will eagerly reccmmend your church to their friends, family members, coworkers, and new neighbors, and why doing so can gain more traction than invitation.

• And last, how to take hospitality beyond Sunday mornings and into the rest-of-the-week workplace, modeled by staff and key laity in a way that creates an irresistible culture of welcoming.

But first, well, first impressions.

We are often reminded that we only get one chance to make a first impression. While the saying is true, many churches—perhaps yours—give little attention, or the wrong attention, to first impressions in the church world, at least in specific terms that lead to practical, doable, repeatable, and teachable behaviors. Still other churches put considerable effort in making sure they have recruited, trained, and deployed the right people in the various functions of hospitality. Some churches even name their hospitality ministry the First Impressions Team.

In the classic *Emotional Intelligence*, groundbreaking author Daniel Goleman talks about the "cognitive unconscious" research showing that "in the first few milliseconds of our perceiving something we not only unconsciously comprehend what it is, *but decide whether we like it or not*" (New York: Random House, 2006, pp. 18, 22; emphasis ours).

Relax. Your first impression won't make or break your church. It takes a whole lot more than hospitality to do that. As Abe Lincoln is thought to have said, "I don't like that man; I must get to know him better." People who have a bad first impression will often get over it and see things more deeply and in a different light than their original observation.

But creating that good first impression increases the likelihood that a first-time attender will return a second time. Many pastors unrealistically assume this good first impression will just happen because people are nice and their church is friendly. It is precisely because of the temptation to treat first impressions casually, almost incidentally, that the first component of a culture of hospitality is intentionality. How intentional is your church in providing great hospitality?

Intentionality is the frame of the bicycle; it is the structure that supports everything else. Intentionality means that (a) the organization (local church or judicatory) has designed and developed a carefully thought-out system to deliver great hospitality, and (b) individuals within the organization are intentional about personally taking the initiative and responsibility to create a culture of hospitality. We will talk more about both as we go along.

Church Hospitality (an organization whose online presence may be found at www.churchhospitality.us) reports their research indicates the number one reason first-time guests don't return is because of poor hospitality. They go on to say that with good hospitality you can increase your first-time attender retention quotient from the national average of 15 percent (11 percent for mainline churches) to significantly more . . . if you follow their process. Their claims may or may not be true, but there is a difference between doing the *functions* of hospitality well (greeting, parking lot welcome, ushering, warm and friendly welcome extended by leaders and Sunday school teachers, and so on), and *creating a culture of hospitality* within the church.

Both are important, and this book's purpose is not only to help local churches excel at improving the functions but also to create a congregation-wide culture of hospitality in these churches. The content is based on two successful teaching tools I (Jim) used while growing my church from five hundred to over four thousand over a period of nearly eighteen years. These are techniques I have now taught to thousands of church leaders in seminars, workshops, and Sunday worship settings.

The tools are not unique to or original from me. I stumbled upon them years ago and have tweaked them and developed a teaching technique to the best advantage in a local church setting. In short, I've simply *packaged* these time-tested, successful methods of hospitality so they can be easily received within the church. There are other tools out there that are just as effective, and you probably already have some kind of system or process in place. Even so, in this book you will learn the advantage of creating a culture of hospitality: *every member, every Sunday.*

The advantages of these two tools are that they are easy to remember and implement, simple to repeat and reinforce, and fun and engaging. All of these are essential to creating culture. And the tools work!

It does not help to give people tools that are too hard to use. Doing so weighs down the toolbox and makes it too heavy; people can't use the tools inside. It also does not help to give people tools that don't work. Unfunctional tools decimate morale and cause people to give up emotionally. So let me reassure you—the tools that are described in this book work.

The first tool is for the purpose of creating a culture of hospitality and is called the 5-10-Link rule. The 5-10-Link rule is one of many systems used in churches today. It is not unique or original to us, as it was developed by Bruce Scott, author of Ministry Toolbox (ministrytoolbox.com).[1] The second tool is what we use to teach hospitality teams how to strengthen the functions of hospitality (greeters, ushers, parking lot attendants, and so on). It is called the W.E.A.V.E.

During worship services and at seminars and workshops, we distribute a small business card–size card with the 5-10-Link rule printed on one side, and the W.E.A.V.E. on the reverse side. (See p. 16 for where to access the card online.) We encourage people to

---

1. 5-10-Link Rule used with permission. Copyright Bruce Scott, President, Church Growth Resources, www.ministrytoolbox.com.

keep the card with them—put it in their Bibles, wallets, or purses. We ask them to learn the material, remember it, and practice it every Sunday! The card forms the basis of the first section of this book, and beginning with the next chapter, we will show step-by-step how to use it.

We have been talking about the frame of our bike: being intentional about creating a process and culture of hospitality. Now we move to the subject of the next chapter, introductions, and discover the often untapped power when church folk take the initiative to introduce themselves to new people. This is the pedal part of our metaphor. People taking the initiative to meet new people is the effort expended, the driving force that makes the church go. There is power in introducing ourselves to others!

In school we learned a romanticized version of the power of introductions through literature, like knights of old in armor extending an open hand to show they held no weapon. In more recent years we have minimized the power of introductions, so that people frequently have interactions with others without ever making an introduction . . . or a connection.

We are about to fix that!

SECTION ONE

GAINING BALANCE AND MOMENTUM

Chapter 1

The Power of Introductions

Get a bicycle. You will certainly not regret it, if you live.
—Mark Twain

I (Jim) love introductions. While I've heard variations of this story, my favorite is as follows:

A pompous old preacher of First Methodist Episcopal South Church in St. Louis—the tall steeple church of the day—introduced the famous humorist Mark Twain at the opening of an impressive new civic library. All the high-society people of the area were there, including prominent politicians, local politicians, and business leaders. Wanting to soak up all the stage time he could, the preacher solemnly strolled back and forth across the platform, plunged his hands into his pockets in a ponderous way, and exhorted: "I submit to you tonight, that we should enjoy a unique experience . . . we will hear from a humorist who should be funny." A few in the crowd chuckled.

Mark Twain bolted onto the platform and mockingly imitated the pompous old preacher, plunging his hands into

13

his pockets and strolling back and forth. The crowd roared when he mimicked, "Friends, I submit to you tonight that you will be a part of two unique experiences. First, you will hear from a humorist who will be funny. Second . . . you've just seen a Methodist preacher with his hands in his own pockets!"

I love Mark Twain. As a matter of fact, on my first date I went to Mark Twain's cave in Hannibal Missouri. I was living near Quincy, Illinois, at the time and had just gotten my driver's license. Do you remember your first car date? When you and your date were alone, with no parents or older sibling to chaperone?

I picked up my sweetheart and drove across the Mississippi, where we were going to spend the day together, just the two of us. Our first stop was to tour Mark Twain's cave. Hundreds of people waited outside for the gates to open. We were divided into little groups, each with a guide. When our time came, we followed the guide through the cavern, squeezed in like sardines, but we didn't care. We held hands, and, like all young lovers, we were in our own world, oblivious to the crowd. We heard the guide drone on about stalagmites and stalactites as we wandered along.

Finally we came to a large space. The guide stopped and explained that this was the very room where Huck Finn and Injun Joe and Becca frolicked and played. "But," said the guide, "when they were here, they had only the light of torches." He continued, "You are in the darkest dark humanly possible; you didn't notice it because of the fluorescent lighting along the cave walls as you toured. But imagine how dark it was in Mark Twain's day. I'll show you. I'm going to turn out the lights, and you will experience total darkness." And he turned out the lights. "I'm going to warn you," he said. "In a few moments when I turn the lights back on, you will be shocked! Your eyes will be shocked trying to adjust."

On and on the guide went, as we stood there in the darkest dark humanly possible. I got to thinking, "We are in a dark room. I am with my girlfriend. What the heck?" I decided to do it. I let go of her hand, slid my arm around her shoulder, pulled her close, and there in the darkest dark imaginable, I stole my first kiss! I remember it still. It was like cave heaven!

And then suddenly the lights came on. The guide was right: I was shocked! My girlfriend was shocked! But not nearly as shocked as the woman I was kissing!

I learned two things that day. Never, ever, go to a dark cave for your first date, and never, ever, be surprised or shocked at what the light of Christ reveals when it shines on us, in us, and through us!

- If we are not careful, in the darkness of our daily living, we might be cuddling up to actions and behaviors that would make Jesus Christ blush.

- If we are not careful, in the darkest places of our soul, we might be embracing mean-spirited attitudes and prejudice that cause hurt and pain to others and ourselves.

- In the darkness of our own hearts, we get cheek to cheek with negative, morale-destroying internal assumptions, like "I'm not good enough"; "I've messed up my life too much"; "I'm not smart enough or attractive enough"; or, "I've messed up my life too much for even God to do anything about it."

- In the darkest darkness of our secret places, we can fall to the temptation to snuggle up with ideologies that separate and divide us and close the doors of healthy relationships.

But the good news is that the light of Christ can shine on us and in us and through us. Once we are introduced to this light, we see

15

ourselves and our world in a whole different way, and we experience forgiveness, acceptance, and a new future.

That's why I love introductions! Isn't it the job of the church to introduce people who live in some kind of darkness to the light of Jesus Christ? Let's not fool ourselves. All around us there are people who are living in darkness.

- Maybe it's your neighbors who have just moved in from out of state. They miss their family and wonder how they are going to raise the kids without family close by.

- Maybe it's your coworker who is living with some guilt or unresolved conflict that is weighing her or him down.

- Maybe it's a family member or close friend who has lost all sense of meaning or purpose.

- Maybe it's those nearly invisible folks who live homeless on the street or who may be struggling with addiction or battling uphill just to survive.

The truth is, there are many people who live in some kind of darkness, and *you* may be the bridge over which they walk to encounter the light of Christ for the very first time! But it is unlikely you can become that bridge unless you first build a relationship with each of those people.

Fortunately that relationship bridge may well be built within the walls of your church. So relax; this book does not intend to fire you up to go door-to-door and ask people if they know Jesus. Instead it seeks to motivate you and equip you to build a relationship bridge when people come to the church for the very first time.

That's right! Those people who live in some kind of darkness may walk through the front door of your church on a Sunday morning, and many of them are pushing their bikes because of

16

some kind of personal flat tire or chain coming off or handlebar getting loose.

- We never know if that person who walks through the front door for the first time on a Sunday morning walked through the door of his or her home on Wednesday afternoon and found a note on the table that read, "I don't love you anymore. I'm outta here."

- We never know if that person who walks through the front door for the first time on a Sunday morning went to the doctor on Thursday morning and heard a dreaded diagnosis: cancer.

- We never know if that person who walks through the front door for the first time on a Sunday morning was up all night on Saturday trying to get his or her kid out of jail.

We just never know what kind of darkness surrounds a person who walks through our doors. And many people—perhaps most people today—who walk through the doors of our church are driven there by some personal pain or hurt or anguish or life-stage change. Don't assume they are "just church shopping" and treat them casually (a very typical church behavior).

This book is about hospitality. This chapter and the next begin our discussion about the second component of a culture of hospitality: relationship. Relationship is the wheels of the bike that allow it to go and that make for a smooth ride!

The two wheels of the bike operate in relationship to each other. One wheel in a culture of hospitality is the circle of friendships *within* the church that members so deservedly love. The other wheel is that circle of acquaintances and friendships *outside* the church that are yet to be made. When the two function together, we experience a smooth, sweet ride!

For a bicycle, the back wheel is the driving force. It gets the energy generated by the pedals and turns that energy into power, which turns the back wheel and thrusts the bike forward. The front wheel is connected to the handlebar and provides direction. In the church, the driving force is the back wheel of relationships yet to be made *outside* the congregation: the mission field! The congregation and its leadership can and must provide the strategic direction, but the driving force must always be to meet new people and meet new needs, and to be thrust constantly into the mission field.

When bicycles were first invented, the wheels were simply metal rims. One of the first great innovations in cycling came with the advent of the pneumatic tire, a tire inflated with air circling that old metal rim. The result? A smoother ride! The problem? Flat tires caused by punctures and blowouts. The fix? Tire pumps and inner tube patches for repairs.

Most everyone knows the feeling of air going out of a relationship; it leaves us feeling flat. Too many churches seem to be limping along with a flat tire, unable to grow, because the spirit of hospitality is either nonexistent or confined to only the circle of friendships *already existing* within the church. Both wheels are needed for a bicycle—or a church—to go! Our hope is that this book will pump up the enthusiasm for a smoother hospitality ride in your church, creating a culture that rides on relationships.

So this book will teach how hospitality is not simply about being warm and fuzzy and friendly, as important as that is. It will also teach about hospitality's deeper duty: to develop relationships and make connections. To connect with one person and facilitate connecting that person to another. To create an environment where people connect to each other, to the church, to the wider world, and to God.

Hospitality is all about connecting! But the doorway to connection is relationship, and relationships begin with introduction. So this section is first about creating a culture of hospitality based on introductions. Second, you will find practical application, tools, and techniques to create that culture in your church.

A culture of hospitality happens when *every person, every Sunday* is intentional about making connections: connecting to someone they do not already know; connecting one person they meet to yet another person; connecting people to God through their intentionality, behavior, and life. In short, when people make themselves available in this way, they can become the bridge over which someone may walk to experience the light of Jesus Christ for the first time.

"Reaching the mission field" gets much attention in churches today. But let's recognize that there are three mission fields:

- The mission field of *the self.* This happens when we truly are so motivated by the gospel that it changes us from passive to proactive, from a consumer to a producer of ministry, and from nonchalant and random to focused and on target.

- The mission field of *the church.* Your church. My church. Before we try to reach the mission field "out there," we must own that the culture in most churches needs to be reached and transformed. Has the culture in your church become weakened by a maintenance mode and become inwardly focused? If so, you need to give as much attention to changing the church culture to one of growth and intentionality, as to attempting to change the community in which the church is located.

- The mission field of *the community.* This is where it's at— where the action is, where we are called to be and to serve! But first, we in the church must be willing to change our culture so we can connect with the needs of the mission field. We must rediscover our biblical roots and create a church DNA that is outwardly driven, not inwardly focused. The community may well begin in our immediate neighborhood, but will quickly expand to include meeting more needs for more people in places all the way to "the ends of the earth."

To best reach the mission field, we have to engage and connect with people. To do this we must create a culture of hospitality. So first, a word about that culture: "Offer hospitality to one another without grumbling" (1 Peter 4:9 NIV).

Overheard at a hospitality training workshop: One usher whispering to another, expressing his hesitancy about the concept of a culture of hospitality, "It was my turn to be friendly last week!"

Culture travels on our words. So we must be careful about the wording we use to refer to hospitality. For instance, do the people in your church see the first-time attender as a *visitor* or as a *guest*?

The Guest/Visitor difference: Highly anticipated, eagerly awaited, exceedingly loved!

A visitor is like this: You're home at the end of a hard day, getting comfortable, settled into your favorite chair, when the doorbell rings. Startled, you look over to your spouse and ask, "Are you expecting somebody?" He or she shakes his or her head no, and both of you scramble around, straightening up the coffee table as you edge toward the door. You look through the peephole to see who is outside. You really are not excited about this visitor at your door.

A guest is like this: You invite somebody over for dinner or dessert or to watch the Cowboys in the Super Bowl! You are excited about him or her coming over; you've cleaned, made special preparations, and are eager for that person to arrive. You've sent him or her directions to your house. As the time draws near, you stand near the door, opening it occasionally, looking out in anticipation. When your guest arrives, your expectations are fulfilled. You experience his or her arrival not as an intrusion or inconvenience but as a welcomed occurrence.

Creating a culture of hospitality includes changing not only our mind-set but also our vocabulary. We need to upgrade "Visitor Registration Pads," "Visitor Parking" signs, and anything else that has the word "visitor" on it. Upgrade the wording to "guest." Say it, speak it, preach it, and teach it.

The "Guest/Visitor difference" is characterized in many ways in seminars and workshops by many presenters—most often as I (Jim) shared above. However it is characterized, I've noticed that it boils down to this: A visitor may well enjoy her or his visit, but a guest will *connect* with the experience of the Sunday morning environment. A guest will experience more than just good feelings; the events will somehow connect on a personal level. And that connection is what increases the likelihood of that person returning for a second time.

I experienced this upgrade personally on a recent Sunday when I attended St. Luke Community UMC in Dallas, our largest African American congregation. As I was pulling into the parking lot, another car parked nearby. The driver got out, immediately walked over to me, extended his hand, and introduced himself: "Good morning. I'm Vance."

I explained that I am a friend of the pastor and wanted to come be in worship with him. Vance took me by the elbow and graciously escorted me to the pastor's office. When I finished my short visit to say hello to my colleague, I exited the office. Vance was right there, waiting for me. "Let me take you to my favorite place to sit in the sanctuary, where you can see everything and the sound is great!"

He seated me next to a delightful elderly lady, who in friendly fashion introduced herself and started making conversation. I commented on her beautiful hat: "I love your hat; it reminds me of when I was a kid and all the ladies wore hats to church."

By the time services were over, she had brought a whole parade of women to me to show me their hats. Throughout the service people made connections, and even the structured greeting time was enthusiastic, genuine, and respectful.

You see, I was not a visitor in St. Luke Community UMC. I was an honored guest in the house of the Lord! I experienced a culture of hospitality that was intentional, robust, and heartfelt. I was *highly anticipated, eagerly awaited, and exceedingly loved.*

No matter what else your hospitality involves, no matter how you go about teaching it and setting up a system or process to implement it, you must answer these questions:

- How are we conveying to our guests that they are *highly anticipated?*

- How are we demonstrating to our guests that they are *eagerly awaited?*

- How are we convincing our guests that they are *exceedingly loved?*

Your answers will be tweaked to your church's specific context, culture, and setting at any given time in its life cycle. But any church can do it, and every church must do it to remain relevant in this world in which there is so much competition for people's time.

Highly anticipated means a lot of thought and preparation have gone into hospitality ministries, which should be evident to first-time guests as soon as they arrive at the parking lot. We communicate that we anticipate guests when we have signage that is good and clear, when the property and facilities are clean and cared for, when nurseries are spotless and sparkling, and when the right people are in the right places to answer questions, relieve anxieties, and ensure everyone of having a good experience of welcome and friendliness.

Eagerly awaited refers to the attitude of the church regarding new attenders. Not only are hospitality teams well trained and ready, but so are regular folk in the congregation. They can't wait for church (not just the worship service) to begin so they can meet new people. Some churches hold short team meetings for their assigned hospitality crew to gather for prayer, last-minute instructions, and a final "rah rah," like a basketball team taking the court. Other churches do it in other ways, but the idea is to display genuine feeling that you can't wait to show Christ's love to anybody and everybody who comes through the door.

Exceedingly loved reflects the kind of love found in 1 Corinthians 13. It simply means that everything we do, we do out of love for them—with no expectation that they will love us back, or even come back; with no intention of getting anything in return, or even getting them to return. It is a holy love for other people the way Jesus Christ loves us. It is grace freely offered in gushing ways—the grace we've experienced along our spiritual journey, overflowing into the lives of others regardless of who they are or where they are in their spiritual journey.

Almost all churches receive more first-time attenders than they realize. These guests may never sign the register, but they are there. A young couple comes to watch their neighbor or coworker's child be baptized. A teenager comes to watch her best friend sing a solo on Youth Sunday, and she brings her parents. A young boy in the confirmation class has invited all his lawn-mowing customers to Confirmation Sunday, and a few will actually come to be supportive.

Every year hundreds of thousands of people attend a church for the first time. The question is, will they come a second time?

Today, a high percentage of first-time attenders walk through the door of the church not because they are church shopping, as in days long gone. They come because they are driven by some significant life-stage change or human hurt or need.

You may be the bridge over which they walk for the first time to encounter the light of Jesus Christ.

How we smile at the person we don't know, make eye contact, go out of our way to introduce ourselves and then to connect that person with other people—how we live out and create a culture of hospitality can make all the difference in the world to a hurting person.

Hospitality has the great quality of producing joy both when we receive it and when we practice it! Hospitality is certainly something we all enjoy when we experience it, as we are reminded in the New Testament: "Gaius, whose hospitality I and the whole church here enjoy, sends you his greetings" (Romans 16:23 NIV).

As important or more important than how first-time attenders sense they are being perceived and treated is simply, how does your church perceive that person who walks in the front door for the first time? When the church's culture is such that first timers are guests— highly anticipated, eagerly awaited, and exceedingly loved—it reinforces the church's relationship with people in the mission field. This is a culture shared church-wide and goes well beyond simply having a hospitality team that does its job well.

Pastors and church leaders must remember that to create a culture of hospitality, they must buy into the concept and commit to:

1. Regularly teach hospitality to the entire congregation in worship settings

2. Model the hospitality desired from congregants

3. Reinforce congregational training by teaching it in staff development and committee orientation meetings.

I (Jim) have done hundreds of trainings on hospitality, and I'm amazed at how many churches try to have hospitality without focusing on introductions. The longer it takes to make an introduction, the less lively the hospitality. Hospitality starts with introductions, but if that is where it stops, you will see interactions without engagement and you will not see the desired outcome: connections.

We now turn our attention to getting beyond introductions and to beginning to truly make connections.

Discussion Questions

1. Talk about a negative first impression or experience you've had. It doesn't have to involve a church. The setting could be anywhere—a restaurant, retail store, gym, dentist, or other location.

   a. How did that experience impact your relationship with that establishment?

   b. Moving forward, did it impact your experience with other, similar establishments?

   c. Did you tell others about your negative experience?

   d. If a friend shared a negative experience from some place, would you be any less likely to try that place yourself?

2. Talk about a positive first impression or experience you've had (again, not just focusing on church experiences but set anywhere).

   a. How did that experience impact your relationship with that establishment?

   b. Moving forward, did it impact your experience with other, similar establishments?

   c. Did you tell others about your positive experience?

d. If a friend shared a positive hospitality experience from some place, would you be more likely to go to that place yourself?

3. What kind of first impression, first-visit experience do people have at your church?

   a. How do you know this?

   b. Is it consistent from week to week, special event to special event?

   c. What was *your* first impression during your first visit to your church?

Chapter 2

Beyond Introduction: Connection

On riding a bike: "I finally concluded that all failure was
from a wobbling will rather than a wobbling wheel."
—*Frances E. Willard*

In the last chapter we talked a lot about the culture behind hospitality. In this chapter we'll turn to the practical application. That is, how to "practice hospitality" (Romans 12:13 NIV).

Never underestimate the power of introductions! Isn't our mission really about introducing Jesus Christ to people in need of the light of his love? We practice hospitality not so we can be friendlier than the local Rotary Club but because doing so gets us ready for the big game: introducing people to Jesus Christ!

Let's practice some hospitality and learn the power of introductions, which lead to the desired, fruitful outcome: making connections.

Look closely at the 5-10-Link card.

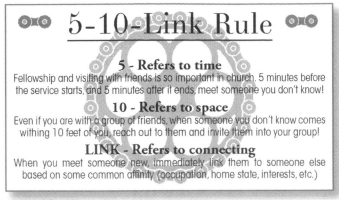

Front of card

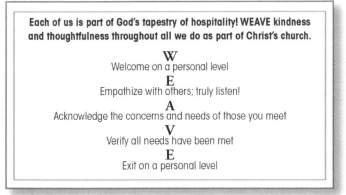

Back of card

The 5 of the 5-10-Link rule has to do with time. It states that for the first five minutes *before* the service begins and for the first five minutes *after* the service ends, you will intentionally find someone you do not know and extend a hand of friendship.

Now, please don't be alarmed!

Visit http://www.cokesbury.com/forms/digitalstore.aspx?lvl=free+downloads to download a free PDF of printable versions of the 5-10-Link and W.E.A.V.E. cards. Password: nqZS59sgUx

This is not to suggest that you shouldn't have good friends and want to spend genuine catching-up time with them on Sunday morning. Maybe you haven't seen your friends for a week or two; it's expected that you would want to spend a lot of time with them. Community in the church is all about friendship! It's great to find friends and huddle up with them and share in close relationships.

But unfortunately for many people in many churches, that's *all* that happens, and then the chances are that your church will not be open and welcoming and hospitable to newer people. This doesn't mean we are unfriendly or cliquish or that we want to build walls difficult for newer folks to penetrate. More often than not, it happens for reasons that have to do with habit and routine that result in good folks not being intentional about meeting new people.

So, how can we find the balance? It's okay to spend ample time to be with close friends, but we must also set aside intentional time to meet and greet people we do not know. This must become a church-wide commitment if we are to develop a culture of hospitality.

This is a big step, and a big commitment on the part of the church. This 5-10-Link intentionality is a covenant that people make with each other. It is intended to change long-ingrained behaviors. This cannot be done lightly, and it cannot be done without regular reinforcement by the pastor and lay leaders.

This is culture change. Everybody in the congregation, every week, covenants that for the five minutes before the service begins and for the first five minutes after it is over, we will intentionally find someone we do not know and introduce ourselves.

For many people, especially in mainline churches, the thought of practicing intentional hospitality after the service ends may seem a bit strange. Most churches are used to thinking of greeting and welcoming and hospitality before the service starts, but some of the most effective hospitality occurs after the service ends.

Consider this: a family who has come for the first time has

ideally had a good experience, listened to a good message, enjoyed great music, and felt a movement of the Holy Spirit. But as they are walking away, when they are primed to share their experience with someone else in some positive way, they go out alone. This dilutes the experience that they've just had.

The 10 of the 5-10-Link rule has to do with space and distance. It states that when you are huddled up with your close friends, enjoying conversation, and you see someone you do not know *walking alone* within ten feet of you, you will intentionally break from your close friendship group, go to that person, and extend a hand of greeting or enter into light conversation. The key is not only to introduce yourself to that person but also to bring him or her back and introduce him or her to your friends. The goal is to make a connection! The exception would be if a person walking alone is deeply immersed in texting on his or her cell phone.

The link of the 5-10-Link rule has to do with linking people, connecting them to others of common or similar affinity. Here is an example: After you introduce yourself to a new person named Abby, you have a brief conversation and discover she is a pilot with Southwest Airlines. You then link her—maybe walking her across the room or hallway—with your friend Brian, who is a flight attendant with Southwest. "Brian, let me introduce you to Abby; she's a pilot with Southwest." This link may lead to a connection that may turn into a friendship that may become a key motivator for Abby to return to the church for a second time.

The link is essential. While it is good to introduce yourself to someone else, that does not create a culture of hospitality. Lots of introductions may lead to lots of interactions, but that does not necessarily lead to lots of connections. What really makes your introduction great is when you immediately introduce or connect the person you've just met to someone else. The best introduction leads to connection. That is, after all, one of the underlying purposes of the church: to connect people to God, to a community of faith, and to the mission field. This starts with connecting people to each other!

When church members see hospitality basically as being warm and friendly, they tend to stop with simply introducing themselves. But when they grasp that hospitality is about far more than courtesy and customer service and is, in truth, about connection, then we have the beginnings of culture change.

If "connecting" is to authentically become part of your culture, let this 5-10-Link rule help you accomplish it in concrete practice. It will help you ramp up the culture in the congregation in a vibrant, contagious way. It will result in changed behaviors and changed hearts.

When practicing the 5-10-Link, you are beginning to establish behaviors that will hopefully lead to new friendships. It is often said that "people don't just want a friendly church; they are looking for a church where they can make friends."

Bicycle riding is really a solitary endeavor, but amazingly, once we learn to ride, we tend to want to ride with others. Whether with a friend alongside for a quick trip, or with a group in a 10k or long-distance race, the exhilaration that comes from riding is multiplied when shared with others. In much the same way, people are intuitively looking for friends to ride with, even when exploring a new church.

Let's be realistic. During a thirty-second introduction, you might be able to shake a hand, share your name, and perhaps learn the name of the person that you are meeting. You cannot realistically form a friendship in this amount of time; friendships are not formed in thirty seconds. But, as many people who teach in the field of hospitality have observed, it is also impossible for a friendship to start without the first thirty seconds! Don't let this opportunity slip by! Have your radar on, and be looking for ways to open the possibility of a new friendship.

A critical caveat must be mentioned here. When you are practicing the 5-10-Link rule, you are being intentional to introduce yourself, make connections, and be friendly and hospitable. Well done! But remember this very important social cue: when you introduce yourself to people you do not know and they in return give you their names, they are telling you they are open to a conversation and maybe even a friendship. They are willing to ride along with you for a few minutes.

On the other hand, sometimes with a big smile you extend the hand of friendship and introduce yourself. The other person just smiles pleasantly and says something like, "Good morning," or, "Nice to see you." What he or she is telling you is: "I need my space; I'm not interested right now in getting to know you." This doesn't mean that person is not a nice person or that he or she is crabby, mean-spirited, or rude. But for whatever reason, at that time the person does not want you in his or her space. It's absolutely critical to respect the personal/social space of another person, so honor that.

The way to honor that is simply to return the smile with a pleasant, "Good morning," and politely move on. Perhaps the only thing worse than an unfriendly church is one that is too friendly! In some cases, over-the-top-in-your-space overtures shout out: "Fresh meat! Get 'em!"

But talk to most people who attend a church for the first time, and they will likely describe their experience not with words like "overly friendly" but rather like, "No one spoke to me. I tried to make eye contact and people seemed to avoid me."

The problem was simply poor hospitality.

What About Names?

Most of the time, most of us don't want to appear unfriendly. So why don't we good church folk naturally introduce ourselves and make more connections? Although the typical church member characterizes his or her church as very friendly, first-time guests routinely report that the church they are checking out doesn't seem so.

True, some folks are just not wired to be outgoing and friendly. Some are natural introverts or are painfully shy. People can only be who they are, so we must give permission for some to be less outgoing than others. That's okay! But even for the less outgoing, the 5-10-Link techniques can help raise the hospitality quotient a little and can give people the tools to not to panic in difficult or awkward situations that might necessitate them getting out of their comfort zone. Read on.

Most people aren't painfully shy, but at times people lack the tools to get over the awkward situations that sometimes arise in the context of church and hospitality. Or they have tools that are too hard to use. Or they have tools that are not helpful. The 5-10-Link provides easy-to-use tools that are likely to lead to success.

Let's apply these tools to tackle the biggest obstacle to hospitality for any church. Fortunately, this obstacle can be overcome with just a little intentionality. It is similar to getting over the fear of riding a bike when you were just learning.

It's this whole thing of names. We just can't remember names! This comes as no surprise to anyone reading this book because, after all, all of us know what it's like to forget someone's name. In this high-pressured, fast-paced, frenetic world, our brains are fried much of the time. There is nothing wrong with not remembering names; it doesn't mean we're not attentive, or we're impolite or rude. It is just a reality.

The good news, however, is that everybody else knows it's a reality. Many of us have a hard time remembering names, and we all know others do as well. There is no problem with not remembering names. The problem comes when we allow forgetting a name to prevent us from making a connection!

But what happens is that most of us feel awkward when we cannot remember a name. Don't you? Especially when we think we *should* remember the other person's name, or when we recognize his or her face but can't put his or her name to it at the moment. When we forget, we sometimes panic, or get angry or frustrated with ourselves.

33

Participants in our workshops frequently say to us: "Honestly, I see people all the time who come to the same worship service I attend, but they sit on the other side of the sanctuary; we've probably met once or twice and I know their faces, but I just can't remember their names. It's embarrassing, so I end up avoiding them or just smiling and saying, 'Good morning,' while I'm really working hard to act friendly without having any real conversation."

Hasn't that kind of thing happened to you?

Or you may know someone, but you go to different Sunday school classes or are in different small groups. Occasionally you see each other at meetings or other functions but can't recall his or her name. Awkward! So when you forget and are embarrassed about asking his or her name, you may settle for surface-level conversations: interactions without engagement.

After a while such surface interactions become normal, even expected. And this becomes the culture of the church, not because it was planned intentionally but because it developed by default. You can recognize these churches that have hallways abuzz with interactions but are lacking engagement. Interactions are an important component of hospitality, but if we stop with interaction and don't move quickly to engagement, there is little chance for connection to happen.

What follows are some simple techniques to help you get over feeling awkward about forgetting names. These techniques are intended to help you take a random interaction and turn it into an intentional engagement that might one day lead to a connection.

Practicing the following scenarios can enable you to have the social courage to get out there and introduce yourself, to make a connection and possibly help someone experience the light of Jesus Christ.

Scenario #1

The simplest way of introducing yourself when you are meeting someone for the first time or when you recognize someone whom you may previously have met but don't remember his or her name is simply to extend your hand and say, "Hello. My name is_____."

Most of the time, this works and you will get a reciprocal response. But as we learned earlier, if the person doesn't reciprocate and engage you, then you just smile and pleasantly go on your way.

Some people are more comfortable with something a little less bold, like, "Hello. I don't believe I've had the pleasure of meeting you yet." This is typically a good introduction approach, but occasionally the person to whom you are introducing yourself will respond with something like, "Oh yes you have. You don't remember when you greeted me at the door a couple weeks ago?" This might lead to a feeling of being slighted, so be aware.

Scenario #2

Ahh, how about that awkward interaction when you *know* you *know* the person you are visiting with in the hallway, and you *know* that person *knows* you should *know* his or her name! But after hemming and hawing and shifting back and forth, and racking your brain to reveal the name of this person you regularly see, you just give up and fake it.

So here's an easy thing you can do: Simply say this: "Help me with your name."

This works well because what you are going through is something most everyone goes through; people will most often understand. Simply stating, "Help me with your name" is a social cue that facilitates communication. You will likely get a response like, "No problem; I'm Chelsea; we've met, but believe me: I understand; happens to me all the time." Immediately you'll want to volunteer your name, just in case Chelsea is having the same trouble you are at the moment. Then your conversation will proceed, with no hard feelings.

This also works because many people love to help. Responding to your request for help is a strengthening bond in the life of the church, especially one in which helping is part of the church DNA. When hallways are abuzz with people interacting, engaging with others, and making connections, it is good to hear the word *help* spoken over and over. That in itself builds the culture of the church!

So don't feel awkward about the simple, "Help me with your name." We have taught and demonstrated this hundreds of times in churches across the country, and never once has anyone been offended that we didn't remember his or her name. Just ask. People understand; they've been there themselves many times. They will appreciate your honesty and candor.

Avoid comments such as, "Are you new here?" After all, that person could be a founding member of the church whom you just don't know or whom you don't see in your sphere of influence, and then your question can be offensive. Similarly you should not ask, "Is this your first time here?" The person you're greeting may be a longtime member or a regular attender whom you've just not yet met.

Now let's move to some slightly more advanced uses of the 5-10-Link. Each of these will help you learn someone's name in a non-threatening, comfortable way.

Scenario #3

It's five minutes after the worship service is over, and you're with your small cadre of good friends from your Sunday school class, talking about the hottest new movie, and you realize it's time for the 5-10-Link. So you (a) break from your group to (b) find somebody you do not know and (c) extend a hand of friendship and introduce yourself: "Good morning. I'm Abby."

Good news! She responds by introducing herself: "Hi. I'm

Chelsea." So you know this is a promising situation in which you want to make a connection. You want to bring Chelsea back to your group and introduce her to your friends Brian and Liz. You want to make some connections. But in the ten seconds it took from the time you introduced yourself, learned her name, and started walking her back to your group, you realize you've already forgotten her name!

Be honest now. Don't you often meet someone, hear his or her name, and then promptly forget it? It's embarrassing, but it happens to us all. In the scenario described above, a likely outcome is that Abby might avoid introducing Chelsea to her friends—that is, fail to make a connection—because she feels awkward and embarrassed.

Don't let that stop you! Here's all you have to do. When you can remember one person's name but can't remember the other person's name, then you simply look at the person whose name you *do not* know (or cannot remember) and motion toward the person whose name you *do* know (and can remember) and you say: "Have you met Brian?"

Following acceptable social cues, nine times out of ten, Brian will extend his hand and say, " Hi. I'm Brian." And the other person (Chelsea) will extend her hand and respond, "Glad to meet you. I'm Chelsea."

The person whose name you forgot will give his or her name, and you've still made a connection! And that connection with another person may very well facilitate a connection to an experience of Jesus Christ.

Scenario #4

You are in the middle of Sunday morning conversation with a fellow member who joined you in providing refreshments at yesterday's all-church golf tournament. As you are retelling stories of Saturday's successful fund-raiser, you notice someone you do not know walking within ten feet of you, alone.

Practicing the 5-10-Link rule, you leave your group, walk to that person, extend your hand in friendship, and introduce yourself: "Good morning. I'm Angie." The man reciprocates, appearing appreciative of the overture, and replies: "Hi. I'm Brad." Again, wanting to follow good hospitality, you want to do more than just meet a new person. You know the importance of connecting him with your friend from the fund-raiser!

So you start to walk back to your group, and in the ten seconds it takes to walk back, for some reason—don't laugh; doesn't this happen to you sometimes?—you realize you can't recall *either* name: your new friend's or your older one's! Maybe it's stress, or nervousness, or simply that our minds are so cluttered so much of the time. Whatever it is, you panic, paralyzed!

This frequently happens and causes all of us a few seconds of awkwardness. We are well acquainted with the person with whom we are in conversation, and may truly consider the person a friend, but his or her name has just slipped our minds. Our kids play soccer together; we see each other at the games and consistently exchange pleasantries. Then all of a sudden, when courteous conversation calls for it, we can't recall the name. This is a malady that affects us all—don't be ashamed of it or assume it's just you. When we begin to obsess about the awkwardness of failing to recall the name, it becomes an obstacle in the way of connecting one person to another. Don't let that stop you!

Practice this great way of bringing two individuals—neither of whose names you can recall—together into a connection. (1) Bring them close together; (2) motion to each of them, left hand going toward one, right hand toward the other; and (3) simply say, "Have you two met?"

Nine times out of ten, they both follow social cues learned in childhood, and will extend their hands and introduce themselves. There; you've done it! Not only have you made a connection, but you have also once again lifted both names into your consciousness, and hopefully more forcefully into your memory bank.

Scenario #5

So what about that one time out of ten when names aren't exchanged? Use the magic word *help* and the permission-giving phrase, "Help me with your name." People will share their names, effortlessly and graciously.

When a church covenants to create a culture of hospitality by employing the 5-10-Link rule (or some other equally effective system), this means members will make it a top priority. It means they understand they are not coming to church on Sunday morning only to *consume* a good message and great music during a spiritual hour but also to *produce* the ministry of the church through their own efforts—searching out and taking advantage of opportunities to become the bridge over which someone may walk for the very first time to be introduced to the light of Jesus Christ. (See chapter 10, "Turning 'Consumers' into 'Producers'.")

We practice hospitality not so we can be warmer and friendlier than the local Rotary club—as good as that may be—but to get ready for what is most important! We practice hospitality within the walls of the church for the same reason a football team practices all week: to get ready for the big game! To be ready to introduce someone else living in some kind of darkness to the light of Jesus Christ! Is it any wonder that the church today has lost much of its fervor and zeal and impact in the world? Why should it surprise us that we can't introduce a darkened world to the light of Jesus Christ when we can't even introduce people to one another!

So we practice in our sanctuary or worship center, in our hallways, and throughout our facilities, and when we are ready and prepared and able to be hospitable, God will put a person in our lives whom we—due to our specific personality, relationship, and smile—are uniquely able and equipped to introduce to the light of Jesus Christ that has shone on us, in us, and through us. We start with the

small, routine opportunities afforded in most churches on a some-
what regular basis. When we get comfortable with introductions
within the church facility, then we'll be better prepared for those
life-changing possibilities outside the church's walls.

Scenario #6

The 5-10-Link rule is equally effective *outside* the church walls.
Has this happened to you? You met somebody at church. Maybe
this person attended your Sunday school class, where you talked for
a few minutes, exchanging pleasantries and names, and had a great
time. Then comes Tuesday afternoon, and you are in the local super-
market, pushing your cart down the aisle, when you notice that very
person pushing his or her cart down the same aisle from the opposite
end! Suddenly you flush, and panic overwhelms you. "My gosh! I
can't remember this person's name!" Your mind plays out a multitude
of awkward scenes in which you pretend to remember the name, or
you acknowledge forgetting, or maybe that person can't remember
your name! Who's supposed to start the conversation? On and on. In
your awkwardness you change direction and head to the asparagus!

How is that person likely to perceive you? As a hypocrite.

We all know the awkwardness of meeting somebody that we
know—perhaps even know well—in a context different from where
we would typically interact with that person. Our minds just go
blank when it comes to his or her name. Don't let that stop you from
making a connection! Utilizing these simple techniques to get the
name of another person and have authentic conversation can make
all the difference in the world to someone who, whether we know it
or not, may be living in some kind of darkness.

"Choose one and use one" is the key here. The 5-10-Link rule is
one of many systems of hospitality used in churches today. It is not
unique to or original with us, and there are other ways of teaching and

remembering hospitality that may work just as well. But the 5-10-Link rule is the easiest, simplest, most effective way that we've found. If the 5-10-Link doesn't seem to fit your church, then find a different tool, and use it! The rule is: "Choose one and use one!" Choose a tool that is simple, easy to remember, easy to engage, and fun to do. That's how you go about creating a culture of hospitality in your church.

Too often churches are way too casual with this critical element of congregational life. Church leaders just assume they can find some friendly person in the church to teach others how to be friendly. Or they simply read a denominational tract on hospitality, pass it out to ushers and greeters, occasionally teach it to the hospitality team, and check hospitality off their to-do list.

To create a culture of hospitality, hospitality needs to be the passionate focus of morning worship at least one Sunday each year. This includes both a great sermon on hospitality and specific, step-by-step instructions to congregants that outline what hospitality should look like in your church. The sermon may vary from year to year, but teaching the 5-10-Link should be repeated every year. Only then will it become part of the fabric of the culture of the church.

Teach it often; practice it regularly.

I (Jim) love introductions because they enable us to excel in introducing Jesus to the world. That's the power of introductions! We can introduce people to Jesus Christ, which enables them to live in a more redeemed, effective way than ever before!

Is it any surprise that The United Methodist Church is struggling with identity and influence? If we want to reclaim our roots of introducing the light of Jesus Christ to a darkened world, we must first learn again how to introduce people to each other. Make your church a living laboratory, and practice hospitality and connections week in and week out. "Every member, every Sunday." When that becomes the culture, the church will change.

It is a must to create a culture where those hallway conversations and connections happen, but it is not enough. What will you connect people to? How will their connection be reinforced and strengthened?

Remember those wheels in our metaphor? What keeps them well rounded are spokes—the strategically placed, thin, metal braces that create little resistance, but together prevent the wheel from collapsing in on itself. What are some of those spokes in your church? Laughter, fun, smiles, small groups, service opportunities, Sunday school classes, support services? Without the little things that provide constant and nourishing connections, the biggest thing will collapse!

Discussion Questions

1. Have you ever thought of yourself as a "bridge over which someone walks to be introduced to the light of Jesus Christ"?

2. When discussing new people:

   a. Does your church talk about *guests* or *visitors*—or both?

   b. Is the word *guest* or *visitor*—or both—used in your signage?

   c. Is the word *guest* or *visitor*—or both—used in print materials?

3. How does your church:

   a. Convey that guests are *highly anticipated*?

   b. Demonstrate that guests are *eagerly awaited*?

   c. Convince guests that they are *exceedingly loved*?

Chapter 3

Turning Moments into a Movement: Pastors and Staff

The bicycle is a curious vehicle. Its passenger is its engine.
—*John Howard*

My (Jim's) mother was proud. Beaming throughout the 11:00 worship service, she was visibly pleased and excited to have me sitting right there by her side. Her little boy, who had grown up in this very church, had gone off to the big city of Dallas and grown an impressive church. But today he was back at the family's home church in Illinois.

It was a big day for her. And for me.

She could hardly wait to introduce me to the preacher after the service, and we dutifully waited in the receiving line. Shortly, we got up to the preacher, and my mom—with that beaming

43

smile—introduced me to him with these words: "I want you to meet my son we talk about all the time. He grew up right here in this church, and now he's the pastor of a big church in Dallas!"

"So glad that you could be here this morning. It's good to see you, and we are so proud of your work," he said as he smiled and shook my hand.

And then he turned his attention to another person and went on.

I watched my mother's countenance deflate.

What the minister had said was okay. It was heartfelt; it was true. But as I drove back home to Dallas, I kept replaying that scene in my mind and wondering how that preacher could have made that whole experience better. Perhaps with more connecting?

How about you? What are you thinking right now that the preacher could have done that would've improved that introduction? That connection?

Here are a few possibilities: He could have looked at me and engaged me in a little more conversation. Something like, "Well, tell me more about growing up in this church. I'm new here, but tell me: have you been back here to preach? Do you get back often?" Or he could have said something like this to my mother: "I bet you are so proud of your son! Thank you for bringing him this morning!"

This would've been a little more engaging and conversational. I would have felt more like he was truly concerned about me. Such questions and comments would have acknowledged how my mother felt at what was to her, a momentous occasion.

But just imagine the impact if he had approached it more like this: "I'm so glad you're here this morning, and I am so proud of you. And I'm sure you are so proud of your mother! I can tell you, she is one of the best members of this church! She's a great friend to me, and she means so much to me and to this church. You are a lucky guy to have a mom like her!"

Wow! If he had approached that short moment in that manner,

several dynamics would've been happening. First of all, I would have thought he was an awesome guy who knew, loved, and appreciated my mother. I would have gone from that place and that experience with a highly positive attitude toward him. Second, my mother would have soared in her spirit! She would've felt the glow of being personally affirmed in front of her son by someone she truly admires and respects. This would have meant the world to her. Plus, it also would encourage her to make other personal introductions to the preacher because she had been so affirmed in doing so this time. Third, everyone standing within earshot of that exchange would have gone away with the same feelings I would have had, and my mother would have had. It would have really felt good. And you know what they would do with that feeling? They would share it with other friends! This preacher could have leveraged those few moments into impact that would have lasted long beyond those short introductory minutes. In today's ministry setting, clergy don't have the opportunity or time for long house-to-house visits, nor does our social culture call for or in some cases even allow it.

Capitalizing on leveraging moments to turn them into something bigger, more meaningful, and more value laden increases the impact of any pastor or staff member in the church world today. When we learn to leverage moments that model the behavior we want to see among our congregants, we create a movement in the church!

You'll notice that in the previous three chapters we've been talking about hospitality as a culture on Sunday mornings, exercised by each and every church member. While the behavior of church members is critical, the pastors and staff are essential to creating that culture. It is their role to model the behavior and demonstrate how to leverage opportune moments into a movement of hospitality within the church. This role has to happen with even more intentionality. It is not difficult, but it requires a conscious, intentional effort.

So let's turn our attention to the next two critical areas of hospitality. The first is similar to what we want each and every person doing each and every Sunday but is more staff specific. The second is the hospitality outside the church and worship experience. That is, what happens Monday through Saturday in our hallways and offices, in our meetings and activities?

First, consider the unique opportunity for pastors and staff when it comes to creating a culture of hospitality. There are two broad categories of introductions that happen more than we realize on a Sunday morning, and it is worth spending some time with each:

- One is when an active church member introduces the pastor or staff member to a visiting family member.

- The other is when an active church member introduces a visiting friend, neighbor, or coworker to the pastor or staff member.

Scenario #7

Following the worship service, a church member goes out of her way to introduce you to her mother (or brother, sister, father, or some other family member) who happens to be in town for a family visit. This is gold! It is a great opportunity to create culture and cast vision for the culture you are trying to implement in the church. Yet, too often preachers unwittingly let this opportunity slip by without leveraging it for the value it presents.

Clergy get so caught up in the tough, daily tasks of ministry that we sometimes lose perspective. Every year we have more people than we probably realize who introduce visiting family members. Be very intentional in these responses. These are critical opportunities! Too often preachers assume that since these family members are from out of town and they're not likely to become active members of the church, it is okay to treat them casually (as I was treated back at my home church). This behavior on the part of the pastor or staff teaches the congregation many poor lessons, but you can easily use such opportunities as teaching moments each and every time you are introduced to a member's family.

A similar dynamic occurs when somebody introduces a new neighbor to you or a friend or coworker. Remember when you were a kid and climbed on your bike, headed to the park or the pool? And you wanted to give your buddy a lift? Some bikes had that narrow little tin backseat, but most of the time you figured out how to get your pal to sit crossways on the frame or hunched up on the handlebar. You just wanted your friend with you. Friendships are important to us, and they are important to the church member who is introducing you to a personal friend. Honor this opportunity!

Scenario #8

Imagine you are standing near the door after worship, engaging in conversations and greeting attenders. Brad, an active member, introduces you to new neighbors, Celia and Tyrone, who have just moved in. It may be that Brad actually invited these new neighbors; it's just as likely that Brad didn't invite them but rather happened to see them coming through the front door of the church. In this instance, Celia and Tyrone took the initiative to attend on their own. However it happens that they have shown up, Brad recognizes them and practices the 5-10-Link. After going out of his way to start a conversation, he wants to make a connection by introducing them to you.

Now, this is really gold, and here's why: The fact that Brad was willing to take the time to introduce you to a newcomer means he likes you! So make a mental note (or better yet, write a note) to yourself to remember to contact him and personally thank him for making an introduction. This creates a culture of introduction by reinforcing a behavior you want to see time and time again. Be cautious not to take for granted Brad's initiative. Thank him for it personally, and look for ways to highlight his action publicly during worship and at meetings and church gatherings.

You may also make a note that Brad is a person you may want to recruit for your hospitality/connections team. He has demonstrated a behavior that you hope to see develop throughout the congregation.

Back to our story, where Brad has introduced you to his new neighbors. There are several ways you can respond. Hopefully you're thinking of a few right now. What follows are some suggestions to leverage this golden moment into a movement in the church of a culture of hospitality.

Look directly at Celia and Tyrone and offer your hand in friendship. Of course, smile and say the typical, "I'm so glad you could be here this morning and to meet you!" Make appropriate small talk, such as, "Where are you from?"

"Denver."

"Well, it won't take long to become a Dallas Cowboys fan!"

Continue with simple, inquiring conversation. "Got the boxes unpacked?"

But here is the leverage point. Be sure to say something along these lines, "You sure are lucky to have Brad as your neighbor! I gotta tell you, around here there is nobody more dependable than he is, and I'm sure you'll find him to be a great neighbor!"

The same dynamics that we talked about in the scenario with a family member will happen here. First, Celia and Tyrone will be impressed at how well you know your church member. Second, Brad will soar on your affirmation! (As a side note, it is worth keeping in mind that church members live every week getting beat up in many ways: work issues, family stresses, financial pressures, time stresses, and so on. People get beat up every week. When they come to church, don't miss the opportunity to build them up.) And third, everybody within earshot of that brief conversation will remember it and tell others not only about the conversation but also about you!

There is one critical caveat: never, ever lie, and don't embellish. Never be less than genuine and authentic. People can see right through what is not real, and your attempts to create a positive impression will instead lead to a negative impression that you are a fake and a schmoozer or cheap glad-hander.

Many times the pastor or staff member doesn't really know well the person making the introduction. Doesn't that happen to you often? Then don't pretend that you do! There's nothing wrong with not knowing every member well, as long as you handle it well.

Scenario #9

You are in the receiving line after church and your church member, Don, whom you do not know well, introduces a newcomer. Naturally, you'll engage in small talk as in the previous scenario—how glad you are to meet him or her, and so on.

But here is the leverage point. Direct your attention to the new guest and say, "I don't really know Don all that well yet, but I'm sure he'll be a great neighbor. It means so much to me that he would introduce you! I'm hoping to get to know both you and him better. That's what this church is all about—people getting to know each other, becoming friends."

Of course, most ministers have faced that awkward situation in which a member whose name you do not know at all introduces you to his or her new neighbor. It is still gold!

Scenario #10

If you don't know the name of the member who is introducing the newcomer, don't fake it! There are several ways you can get to

49

the name. Practice the 5-10-Link rule. While this introduction is unfolding, look around and see if there is somebody standing nearby that you *do* know. Here is how it would go:

Traci, who is a member but whose name you do not know (or at least at this moment can't recall), introduces you to her new neighbor, Christy. You don't want to fake that you know Traci, but you also feel awkward that you can't remember her name. So you glance across the hallway and happen to see Brad. Ask him to come over, and say, "Brad, hey, I want you to meet someone here." When Brad joins you, look at the newcomer and say, "I want you to meet one of those kind of church members every pastor loves to have around." Brad, following natural social cues, will extend his hand and introduce himself. "Hey, glad to meet you. I'm Brad." Nine times out of ten, both Traci and Christy will reciprocate and introduce themselves!

What if they don't introduce them selves? If there is nobody around with whom you can practice the 5-10-Link rule, use the magic word. It's perfectly okay to say, "Hey, thank you for bringing your new neighbor to meet me; now help me with your name." Traci will tell you. Then be sure to say something like, "This means so much to me that you brought a friend to meet me. I sure hope to get to know you both better. That's what this church is about—making friends and looking forward to forming deepening friendship."

These scenarios happen week in and week out in churches of all kinds all across the country. Practice them and become comfortable with leveraging individual moments into a movement of hospitality. Practice them regularly, not only on Sunday morning but also in staff settings where together you are sharpening your tools to provide better ministry.

Teach these to both staff and key lay leaders in the church. Let it become second nature in the church and you will create a culture of hospitality! Leverage these precious moments into a powerful movement within the life of the church.

Casting Vision Through Hospitality

One of hospitality's less appreciated but most important characteristics is that it is one of the best ways to cast vision for the culture you want to create! We discuss everything in this section thoroughly in our workshop *Change the Culture Change the Church*, but a few tips here will prove invaluable to you.

First, vision casting is arguably one of the most important jobs of the pastor and staff. How do you cast vision in your church? Many pastors assume the best way to cast vision is through an annual sermon series on the vision and direction of the church or perhaps through powerfully written blogs or a regularly appearing column in the church paper. While both of these are good, and must be incorporated into your vision casting, the best ways to cast vision are through introductions, meetings, and worship. Culture leaks, little by little. Vision to create and maintain culture must be cast continuously.

Our focus here is to cast vision through introductions, which by now you know is the beginning of a culture of hospitality. Every time you—as a pastor or staff member—are introduced to someone or make a new introduction, you have the golden opportunity to cast vision for the culture you want to create. Now we turn to how to go about it.

First, be clear about the culture you want to create. Sadly, for many pastors the organizational culture of their church is the last thing they think about, if they think about it at all. Your culture should be your first priority. When culture is clear, then the laity is unleashed to produce the ministry your church needs to be effective and fruitful. If your culture is not clear, you'll never gain the traction you'd like to get.

The person primarily responsible for setting the culture of any organization is the leader. In the church that person is the senior or lead pastor. If you are the senior pastor reading this, you'll be well served to discern your *culture words*: three or four words or short phrases that capture the culture you would like to live by in your local church. These words should be short, memorable, and easy to teach to staff and laity. For example, Southwest Airlines, famous for its culture, describes "the Southwest Way" as having "a Warrior Spirit, a Servant's Heart, and a Fun-LUVing attitude." Those culture words color everything they do and make clear that it's not what they do but how they go about doing it.

For me (Jim), in my ministry, my culture words are simply: "Creative, Passionate, Relevant." Those words were what set the culture of the church I pastored and the ministry I do today.

Your culture words are yours. They must come from your heart and be authentic to who you are. They may be the same words as your best friend's or some other pastor's, but they have to be true to you. They must come from your heart and ring true to your core being. The idea is that your culture words are not necessarily going to be unique to you, but they must be genuinely you!

To discern these words for yourself, spend some prayerful time alone for self-reflection. As culture words begin to emerge, be sure they are biblically based. Perhaps they will emerge from a favorite biblical story or passage. As the culture words become clearer for you, bounce them off trusted friends—do they really match who you are? Can your friends see this desired culture from you as genuine and authentic?

I (Fiona) am often asked to lead workshops with clergy staff and leadership teams on the subject of culture. It is certainly perceived as an intriguing and seemingly elusive concept—like a "secret sauce." Culture has been held up as the competitive advantage for companies like Southwest Airlines, Whole Foods, and the Container Store, and the results show. I had the brilliant opportunity to work at Southwest Airlines and see their secret sauce in action. I witnessed

Southwest's culture of "Warrior Spirit, Servant's Heart, and Fun-LUVing Attitude" shine consistently.

This culture rallied and united the organization in difficult times and led the celebration of special moments, both large and small. Now at Interstate Batteries, I have the opportunity to be part of the beginning of the journey, as we articulate and mobilize the purpose and values that have been part of Interstate's heartbeat for over sixty years.

Our culture includes words like *team, courage,* and *love.* It's powerful to see the emotional connection people have with these words. At Interstate, the floodgates have opened with stories from our team members, distributors, customers, and suppliers about how the company has touched lives. And this is the battery business!

When I talk to churches about the power of culture and the possibility for transformation, I'm regularly faced with what can only be described as a polite resistance. It usually begins with an earnest, "Yes, but . . ." I think for many of us the concept of culture seems a little, well, fluffy.

Culture is not as tangible as programs, tactics, and campaigns, so we instinctively resist it. What I believe we're missing is the fact that a healthy culture, one that is carefully nurtured and developed, literally breathes life into every aspect of the church, which not only accelerates growth but also feeds new growth.

Once you come up with your culture words, there is a don't and a do ahead of you. *Don't* make a big deal of your words. You don't need to make posters or conduct a big campaign introducing them. This would be unnecessary and counterproductive.

But *do* start using your words in hallway conversations, sermons, articles, meetings, and, most of all, introductions! Be intentional about including one or all of your culture words in the exchange of an introduction—to cast vision constantly!

For example, I would include my culture words (creative,

passionate, relevant) like this when introduced to a member's new neighbor (as in scenarios #7–10): Looking at the neighbor, I would say about my member, "You sure are fortunate to have Joe as a neighbor! I know we're lucky to have him here. We really value creativity, and he is one of those guys who is just so creative with everything he does!"

Or if I don't know Joe well: "I'm sure you'll be glad to have Joe as a neighbor. I don't know him all that well yet myself. But here we really value being passionate, and just that Joe took the time to introduce us shows me he's passionate about making connections in our church!"

Casting vision about the culture you want to create is expressly saying what you value and describing "how we do things around here," over and over until the culture you want to create becomes embedded throughout every part of the church.

Senior pastors, you must invest the time and prioritize teaching your culture words—what they are, what they mean to you, and why you want them to capture the culture of the church—to your staff. Getting their buy-in to use these words and teach them to key influencers in the church is a must. If you can't get their buy-in, you may well have to get new staff members. The buy-in is that this is the culture that as a *unified team* you will develop throughout the church. The bonus—after the pastors and staff begin to cast vision using the culture words—is that the laity will pick up on these words and begin to do the same. That's how culture emanates outward from the leader and becomes embedded into every aspect of the life of the organization.

Unlocking the Bike

Every seasoned bike rider knows the importance of a bicycle lock. Locks come at about any price and in any style, but they all serve the same function. When you stop riding, the safest bet is to lock up your bike so it won't be stolen. But to ride again, you have to unlock it! What unlocks the bike—and hospitality—to enable us to ride is simply intentionality. Everything we've been talking about starts with intentionally thinking about ways we can create a culture of hospitality. Unlocking the bike is the task of the pastors and staff, and is fundamental to unleashing the creativity, energy, and excitement of the laity to generate the movement of the church.

In our metaphor, the third component of a bicycle is the handlebar, which provides both direction and gyroscopic action. When the rider pulls up on the handlebar with the upper torso while pushing down on the pedals with the feet and legs, gyroscopic force is created. It is this delicate interaction that in part explains the mystery of what keeps a bike upright and going! The handlebar is for direction, but it also enables the interaction between the upper torso of the rider and the feet and legs that provide the thrust.

The parallel component of hospitality is interaction. You can't have great hospitality without interaction between people, but that interaction must lead to some kind of forward movement. It is the gyroscopic force of both direction and momentum. This kind of interaction leads to being intentional about turning everyday interactions between persons into something that produces energy and momentum for the church.

Interactions that go nowhere become little more than pleasant exchanges. Casting vision is a great way for pastors and staff quickly to move a random interaction into an opportunity for real engagement. A nondenominational friend describes it like this: "In mainline churches you treat interaction with a new guest like an encounter between people who have been married for many years. You get casual and take so much for granted. In nondenominational churches, interacting with new guests is more like an encounter between people who are still dating. We are intentional about the impression we make and the way we engage."

Pastors, staff, and judicatory leaders set the direction in so many ways, including creating a culture of hospitality. (See chapter 5, "Hospitality in the Workplace.") They must model transforming opportune interactions into true engagement, which produces the energy that moves the church forward. John Wesley said something like this with his admonition not to "trifle," in his "Rules for a Preacher's Conduct." In the parlance of his day, wasn't he saying something about being intentional? About moving interactions forward? My guess is this admonition would extend to interactions at church, including in the hallways of the building or in the denominational office.

Pastors and staff have to unlock the bike. It takes intentionality to move from interaction to engagement. Interaction leads to engagement but is different from it. Like the forward thrust that happens when we pull up on the handlebar while pushing down on the pedals, interaction gets us started. Interaction is a critical piece of hospitality, but it is simply a starting point. Interaction must quickly move to engagement for us to enjoy a smooth ride of any distance.

In many churches there are many interactions between church members and with new people. But because of a lack of intentionality, these interactions seldom lead to engagement. Some churches that any first-time attender would say are unfriendly have a ritualized time in the morning worship service for something like passing the peace or greeting your neighbor. These are designed as interactions, but which many churches mistake for connection. There are plenty of churches with plenty of hallway conversation among members, but again, churches can easily fall into the "friendly talk trap" and mistake casual interaction for true engagement. Interactions that move to engagement lead to connection, which is the subject of the remaining pages of this book.

I (Jim) have heard it expressed like this: Intentionality + Vision Casting + Buy-In = Culture Creation. The main job of pastors and staff is to unlock the bike and allow their congregation to ride! Intentionality is where it starts, and it is the responsibility of pastors and staff to turn moments into the movement that creates a culture of hospitality. I (Fiona) am a layperson who loves to help churches sharpen their culture. You may ask, "What does culture look like in a church?" I believe that a church's culture is visible at every turn—it shows up everywhere from hallway conversations to Sunday morning worship experiences. I sing in the choir at my church and see culture breathe through our community of voices as we lift each other up during challenging times and seasons of new birth and hope.

Culture shows up in laughter and shared jokes, and urgent whispers as we rush along the hallway to the sanctuary, catching up on this week's events. Our culture of hospitality demands that we care for each other deeply, while intentionally reaching out to guests and new members and pulling them in close. These are sacred elements of culture: caring, connecting, and celebrating. We're called as leaders to identify these unique characteristics and invest in cultivating them with much care and energy.

Discussion Questions

1. When and where was the last time you introduced someone? How did it go?

2. When and where was the last time someone introduced you to someone else? How did that go?

3. Share a time when you experienced the awkwardness of not being able to introduce people because you didn't know, or couldn't remember, their names.

4. Do you think name tags help or hinder introductions? Explain.

Chapter 4

Hospitality Teams: Recruiting and Training

Life is like riding a bicycle. To keep your balance
you must keep moving.

—*Albert Einstein*

It was awkward enough that he was talking on his cell phone during morning worship. But he was an usher! Passing the collection plate!

His loud, whispery voice could be heard all the way up to the chancel area, and I (Jim) struggled to contain my anger just moments before I was to preach as a guest speaker. Every attender in his section was visibly disturbed at the sight of this otherwise distinguished-looking middle-aged man holding his cell phone to his mouth with one hand and extending the collection plate with his other hand with a pious smile.

Oh yeah. He made it worse.

When it came time for the two-handed collection plate switch—you know: when the usher receives the plate from one row and then changes hands and sends it down the next row—he actually asked the woman on the end of the row to hold his cell phone, mid conversation!

He apparently caught the eye of the camera crew, because they focused in on him, flashing his multitasking conversation on the screens. All over the worship center, people squirmed uncomfortably, not knowing whether to laugh or boo or ignore what was happening.

That is, until the block white letters scrolled out under his image on the screen: "Good ushers don't do this!" Then everyone burst into laughter as he offered up to the cameras a goofy grin. The scrolling text continued: "If you wouldn't do this, you may be great on our Hospitality Team. Contact _____ to see how you can make a difference in the worship service." It was all a setup. A compelling, funny one at that. And one they didn't want to let the preachers on the platform know about in advance, just for the surprise factor.

Almost every church of any size has fewer hospitality team members than needed. Recruitment is a constant in the life of the congregation. In our training, people frequently ask, "Why is it so hard to get people to do something so simple? Why is it that when people sign up to be a greeter or usher or Connection Center host they may not even show up for their turn?"

This book is not about hospitality teams, in part because churches have so many different configurations of functions carried out by their teams. A mainline church may confine hospitality to ushers and greeters, maybe even parking lot attendants or greeters. Many newer, more contemporary-styled churches include coffee baristas, connectors, hosts, and on and on. No one size fits all, but all need a culture of hospitality! When this culture is present, when the DNA of the church is to be engaging, connecting, uplifting, fun, helping, then it is much easier to recruit people for specific functions.

Before you hope to solve the problems of recruiting and training hospitality team members, look first to the church's culture. Is the church culture conducive to letting desire, willingness, and eagerness to serve emerge organically from the hearts of people? Does it foster the belief that every attender may be the bridge over which a person may walk to be introduced to Jesus for the very first time? Does it promote fun, creativity, and energy when people team up together?

This book is about creating that kind of cultural underpinning for recruitment efforts. You'll see how this happens as you read on. "Recruitment" for some sounds too corporate or militaristic, so they prefer more invitational language like, "Our church is starting its annual campaign of inviting members to consider being a part of the hospitality team." But whether you are "recruiting" or "inviting," here are a few quick tips that church leadership can do to facilitate expanding and energizing your hospitality:

1. Thank volunteers often and regularly! Do this during worship with a compelling narrative, like the following: "Earlier this morning I watched one of our parking lot greeters hold an umbrella over a young family so they wouldn't get drenched coming in. I thought, 'Wow! How thoughtful and how helpful!' Our hospitality team members go out of their way so often. Let's give them a great hand!" These twenty seconds can be leveraged into great benefit.

   First of all, it's true that hospitality team members do great work and often go out of their way to make sure guests feel welcomed. Second, if hospitality is the linchpin of what the church does, then it needs to be acknowledged and appreciated. Third, people want to do what will make a difference, and what they have time to do. Hospitality—compared to being a Sunday school teacher, for instance—requires a small time commitment, but has a great impact. These two values, manageable time commitment and major impact, should be stressed, not by haranguing congregants to "sign up for the hospitality team," but by heartfelt demonstrations of appreciation.

2. Be creative! As the example of the talking usher points out, the people you *want* on your hospitality teams are fun-loving, smiling, positive, and happy folks who have a "do anything to help" attitude. These people don't respond to boring. Vance Havner, the famous evangelist from an earlier day, used to say, "Worse than the blind leading the blind is the bland leading the bland." Hospitality team folks aren't bland; their imaginations aren't captured by the same old stale words and "we need you" approach. But creatively showing the DNA of a fun, lively church will instinctively bring them to the surface if they see that their time investment is truly making a difference.

3. Go and show! Too often, training for hospitality teams becomes counterproductive. A group of folks gather in a room and listen to the presenter talk about the things they should and shouldn't do, and how to do them. Maybe they watch a video from an outside resource, or invite a guest presenter. All this may be good, but it also may unwittingly go against the creative gene discussed earlier.

   In addition, there is great value in taking hospitality team members (as a group or in small groups) to places where they will experience great hospitality. Let them feel it. Let them see how it happens. Afterwards, debrief the hospitality aspect of the event. Together, learn from it; let participants describe what they felt and experienced and how they could replicate that feeling in their own church. In short, they become producers of the ministry, not just consumers of what someone has to teach them. A few examples:

   • Go to a church known for its great hospitality (many churches have Saturday night services that wouldn't conflict with your own Sunday morning duties). Make notes. Pay careful attention to how people are hospitable. Ask questions of people serving in various functions, such as training, scheduling, etc.

- Go to a great hotel for a few hours and wander around, observing the hospitality. Ask employees in the lobby about their training and about their key practices to make guests feel welcome.

- Go to some professional sporting event. Take note of how ventures like a Major League Baseball team or a professional football, baseball, or hockey team have learned to use great hospitality as a means of getting people who come for the first time to return a second time. People return not only because of the product on the field, but also because of their experience enjoying a hospitable environment!

Many times, staff members on the hospitality teams of these ventures are eager to get out to places like churches to share what they've learned about hospitality. They may be doing it for marketing purposes, but your church can learn from them!

Since their invention in 1817, bicycles have constantly improved. Early bikes didn't have pedals; the rider sat on the wooden bicycle and pushed it forward with his or her feet. Then the big-front-wheel, little-back-wheel version appeared, followed by the big-back-wheel, little-front-wheel models. Both of these iterations had the pedal on the front wheel, needing no chain and sprocket. Bikes for girls and women then appeared, to allow females to ride while wearing long skirts. A while later came the chain and sprocket, then pneumatic tires with air to cushion rough rides, then gears to be shifted, and specialty editions like mountain bikes and racing bikes. Newer offerings have smaller tires, weigh less, and have more streamlined frames. Like most things, bikes have continued to improve to meet the demands of a changing society.

If your church is still riding an 1860s or 1970s hospitality bike, you will have a hard time competing with churches whose hospitality has changed and improved exponentially over the years. We encourage you to explore other highly successful churches and venues with great hospitality to see who is riding what kind of bike, and how you might tweak what's happening today to the needs of your church. This will motivate people to be willing to "clip in" and take some risks not only to provide great hospitality but also to create a culture of hospitality.

The W.E.A.V.E.

Look again at that 5-10-Link card (p. 28). On the back you will find W.E.A.V.E., which helps hospitality teams be conscious of the need to weave care and concern throughout the fabric of hospitality. I first used the W.E.A.V.E. when Trietsch Memorial UMC in Flower Mound, Texas, did a major hospitality training event while I was the senior pastor there. The training was led by my friend Michael Tamer, a businessman and corporate trainer. Along with his colleague Scott Thomas, he coined the concept. We found it a great tool for training and equipping hospitality teams. The W.E.A.V.E. is also a great tool for practicing hospitality in the workplace, especially in denominational offices (For more on this, see chapter 5).

W: Welcome on a personal level

E: Empathize; truly listen

A: Acknowledge the concerns and needs of those you meet

V: Verify all needs have been met

E: Exit on a personal level

Again, I (Jim) claim no credit for coming up with this. It is simply a tool that my church discovered and put to good use. Over the past eight years I have taught it to hundreds of hospitality team members in local churches across the country. While probably originally developed for the business world, it has great value for church hospitality teams, pastors, and staff.

W: Welcome on a Personal Level

This doesn't mean that ushers should intrude on the personal space of someone walking in the door. Nikki, standing at the door, shouldn't hand the newcomer a bulletin or program and say, "Hi! I'm Nikki. What's your name?" This approach is too intrusive.

Nikki should be trained to have her radar on. She should do more than simply smile and with rote, robotic tenor say, "Good morning" to everyone walking in. But not much more.

She could say something like (if, for instance, there has been a storm earlier in the morning), "Good morning. Were the roads pretty tough with all the rain?" Or, if someone comes in wearing a Dallas Cowboys sweatshirt, "Good morning. Go Cowboys!"

Wherever appropriate, people who want to create a culture of hospitality will learn that fine balance between being personal and being respectful of personal space, between being friendly and being intrusive.

Practice, practice, practice, and utilize role-play during training.

Wrong: "Wow! That dress sure looks good on you!"

Right: "Good morning. Oh, such a cute baby! How old?"

E: Empathize; Truly Listen

Speaking of the above example of right and wrong, consider the following exchange between a greeter (who would make any preacher proud) and a young couple, probably coming to the church for the first time. The woman held tight to the hand of a toddler; the husband carried a baby in a bulky, plastic carrier.

Greeter: "Good morning." (Looking in the carrier at the baby) "Oh, cute outfit! She looks about the same age as ours." Then addressing the toddler, the usher quickly commented, "I bet you make a good big brother!"

The young family paused briefly just inside the doorway. The mother smiled and replied, "Thank you."

Said dad, beaming, "Yep, he's a good helper."

Then suddenly, the mother commented to no one in particular: "We're having a hard time deciding if he's old enough to go to a funeral."

The greeter, a young mother herself, truly empathized, "Oh, I'm so sorry. Whose funeral, may I ask?"

Mom: "Bill's sister's baby—a little girl, stillborn." She teared up, then caught herself and continued, "Oh, I'm sorry." She said, extending her hand, "I'm Sheila and this is my husband, Bill, and of course our little guy, Ro, and his new baby sister, Chloe."

Bill: "Yeah, it's tough. We weren't expecting it; nobody was, not even the doctor. It was just time for delivery, and something went way wrong. We don't know what to do. They are having a little memorial service for the baby tomorrow morning. My folks are coming in from Iowa; they thought they would be coming to babysit . . ." His voice trailed off.

A: Acknowledge the Concerns and Needs of Those You Meet

The conversation continued like this.

Greeter: "Fortunately I haven't had to face that. I can only imagine it must be so terribly hard. One of my friends in our Tuesday morning mother's group did suffer through a similar tragedy not long ago, though her baby hadn't gone full term."

Sheila: "Well, it's hell; that's all I can tell you. Sorry, I know I shouldn't say that in church, but everybody is in shock, and it is just so terrible."

Greeter: "That's okay. I understand." Motioning to them, she politely asked, "Here; may I introduce you to the friend I told you about? She's probably had some experience with this and might be able to help you sort out your questions about taking Ro to the service."

As the little group walked away from the door to find the friend working the connection center booth, the greeter flagged down another person on the hospitality team to take her place at the door as she escorted Sheila and Bill and their children.

Notice that the greeter could simply and politely have said, "I'm so sorry. We'll be praying for you." And then she could have turned her attention toward other people coming in. But by empathizing she picked up on the emotion behind the hurt and the confusion; she truly listened. And what she heard convinced her that this situation trumped any of her other duties—she acted.

This young couple didn't strike up a conversation with the greeter because they thought she was a pastoral counselor—they just needed to talk. They *had* to talk. Opportunely, this greeter's interest in them personally, in the baby, in drawing a connection between them and her, proved to be the trigger that allowed the conversation to begin.

V: Verify All Needs Have Been Met

When the worship service was over, the greeter returned to her station, rightly guessing that the young family would leave by the same door they came in through. Seeing them shuffling through the crowd leaving, the greeter approached in an intentional way:

Greeter: "I don't know if the service could have been helpful for your heart today, but I wanted to be sure you got to have a good conversation with my friend."

Sheila: "Yes, she was so nice."

Bill: "And helpful, too. She's even arranging for some group in your church to bring a bunch of food over to my sister's house tonight for when everyone gets here."

Sheila: "I wish we had come to the church sooner. The funeral home is providing a preacher to say something at the memorial service, but it might have been nicer to have your pastor."

Greeter: "That's okay. I'm sure one of the pastors can be there, and it will be an honor just for them to be there by your side."

Sheila: "Well, tell everyone thanks. Everyone has been so helpful; we didn't expect anything like this."

E: Exit on a Personal Level

The brief encounter ended like this:

Greeter: "If there is anything at all we can do for you, just let the pastor know. This is such a terrible thing and a tough time for you all. I'm so sorry." She handed Sheila her church hospitality team calling card. "Don't feel obligated at all, but please know I'd like to keep in touch—you are all going through so much. I don't want to interfere, but I'm here for you if you need anything at all."

This vignette is a loving example of the W.E.A.V.E. Who knows? Perhaps this young family (and the sister's family) might soon became members of the church and go on to become leaders in the grief support ministry. It is important to note that this outcome is not why they received radical hospitality. They received it because they were children of God in need of a little kindness in Christ's name. If they had never set foot in the church again, it would have been worth it!

Most examples of the W.E.A.V.E. will be less extreme, but the process is the same, and is just waiting for your creativity. Whether a guest is bringing a concern with them (like the young family above), or has a question about where the child care is or who is responsible for a particular function, ask yourself now how your hospitality teams can employ the W.E.A.V.E. to provide better guest service.

None of what I've just shared is magic. Will you still have to work at recruiting hospitality team members? Sure. Will you still have trouble effectively training hospitality teams? Sure. But implement these, and you'll see it greatly increases the return on your efforts.

Always keep in mind that *culture* is different from the *functions* of hospitality. Almost every church has some way or multiple ways of training those who serve on various aspects of the hospitality team. Sometimes training is self-developed, or sometimes a church purchases a hospitality program from denominational or other sources. Whatever your church's particular method, be sure the process and specifics are built on the W.E.A.V.E.

The point of hospitality teams and the W.E.A.V.E. is to turn random interactions into significant engagement, which is the fourth key component of a culture of hospitality.

The fourth component of the bicycle is the seat—the center of gravity, where the rider sits to engage all the other aspects of the bike. Oh sure, a person can ride without a seat; he or she can ride standing up, as we used to call it. But sooner rather than later, the rider will become exhausted, the pacing will become strained, and the fatigued and frustrated rider will stop, worn-out.

Hospitality teams set the pace for the church's hospitality. They are the trained folks who have a vision of how their efforts turn casual interactions into meaningful engagement, especially with newcomers. They are working toward the kind of engagement that leads to connection. Because they are often the first encounter a first-time guest has with the church, hospitality team members become the center of gravity. Most of what a disconnected newcomer experiences spins around the hospitality team and its functions.

The Top Ten Best Practice Tips for Hospitality Teams

10. Remembering names IS important! We all know the value of calling a person by name. We all know how good it feels when someone else remembers OUR names! When serving on the hospitality team, keep a small notebook with you and write down the names of new persons you meet. Ask them to repeat and spell the name. Pray for each name during the week. It will help you remember so you might be able to call the people by name when you see them the next time.

9. Whenever possible, when asked the "Where is . . . ?" questions, personally escort the inquirer to his or her destination instead of simply directing him or her to it.

8. Utilize "the hand-off" when it isn't practical to actually escort a person to the destination. Hand the guest off to another person (whether on the hospitality team or not) with a solid introduction: "Steve, please meet Larry; would you show him where the Family Life Center is? Thanks!" This models introduction and connection.

7. Extend hospitality to the parking lots and outside the front doors: greeters with umbrellas on a rainy day are a welcome sight!

6. Provide bright fluorescent vests and walkie-talkies to parking lot greeters, even if the walkie-talkies don't always work. It adds to the professionalism and increases the sense of "feeling safe" for guests when they arrive.

5. Create good culture by extending your church's messaging of upcoming events throughout the building, including in restrooms on stall doors, above urinals, and around mirrors.

4. First-time guests (especially with children) are always interested in safety, cleanliness, and professionalism. Hospitality

includes check-in procedures in the children's areas, eager teachers in place as guests arrive, and freshly cleaned and cared-for classrooms and restrooms. This gives witness to a sense that "somebody has really thought about us here!"

3. Practice "preemptive hospitality" by constantly asking: What do first-time guests need to know? What are their needs? What do they want to experience? What will make them glad they are here? What can we do in hospitality to make them recommend our church to friends?

2. Go out of your way to create the way! There are thousands of websites with excellent information for church hospitality, but nothing will help much unless you really LOVE people and love interacting with people. Lead with your heart and your words, feet, and hands will follow in a hospitable way.

1. SMILE! There is no crying in baseball and no frowning in hospitality!

Discussion Questions

1. Does your church have "culture words," as discussed in this chapter? What are they?

2. Have you experienced "ritualized" time for interactions at a church? Discuss the pros and cons of ritualized time.

   a. What is the purpose of this time?

   b. Is that purpose achieved?

   c. How do you know?

3. Can you think of a time when you have been impacted— positively or negatively—by an interaction you overhead or witnessed at church? Elaborate.

Chapter 5

Hospitality in the Workplace

Toleration is the greatest gift of the mind; it requires the same effort of the brain that it takes to balance oneself on a bicycle.

—Helen Keller

We now explore hospitality in the workplace; that is, the environment of your church throughout the week. You may be surprised to learn that the pedals—the fifth component of the bike—turn here first.

The pedals are what produce the forward thrust for momentum. Located pretty much in the center of the bike, they connect the rider's effort with the mechanics of the bike that turn the wheels that move the gyroscopic forces forward! And in many bikes they also control the brake by pedaling in reverse. The pedals control your speed and give you a sense of control over the environment of the bike.

Hospitality in the workplace—in the church offices outside of worship—is where the culture of hospitality is birthed, nurtured, modeled, taught, reinforced, and celebrated. It will be virtually impossible to create an authentic culture of hospitality on Sunday mornings if the staff and key laity fail to practice hospitality throughout the week in the same way they want it mirrored on Sunday morning. Likewise, if you are in a denominational tribe, the principles in this chapter apply to judicatory offices as well! It is a steep, uphill ride if the judicatory office doesn't model the same hospitality it wants to see exemplified in the local churches.

Before we become adept at making connections in our churches on Sunday mornings, we had better be authentic in how we model this connection in our daily interactions. Again this takes teaching and coaching and reinforcing.

Hospitality in the workplace is not to impress those who wander into our work environment. Rather, it is to impress upon ourselves and reinforce a different way to look at our workplace. The church (or denominational or judicatory) office is not the *place* where we come to work; it is the *space* in which we do our ministry and, in so doing, set the culture for our organization! Healthy organizations operate on the commitment that culture starts at the head and emanates outward to every aspect of the organization. When there is effective alignment, the culture exemplified in a Sunday school class in a local church will reflect the same DNA and culture created and modeled from the judicatory office.

In my work I (Jim) am in many conference and district and other judicatory offices. While most of the time I encounter hospitality that is nice and courteous, way too often the hospitality, or lack thereof, is so poor, the environment so sterile, the atmosphere so cold that there is no way local churches can create the kind of hospitality the denominational execs want them to display!

One of the observations of organizational culture is that it is unlikely the outliers of an organization will behave differently than the head of the organization. This is what great cultures like Southwest Airlines demonstrate to us. What makes their culture so great and so notable is that the bag handler in Amarillo will exemplify the same culture as the CEO in Dallas. This doesn't happen by accident. Wise organizations understand that "culture leaks"—we have to constantly cast the vision and be reinforcing the culture we want.

This key element of understanding and living out healthy culture is where churches fall down so drastically. In our efforts to accomplish our mission, we unwittingly stress out, juggling so many agendas and ideas and directions, that our culture becomes diffused and our people become confused. Cultural clarity is what makes it possible to accomplish our mission, yet mainline churches seem to pay little attention to the most critical element that can lead to our success. One simple, identifiable, visual way to create cultural consistency and clarity is through hospitality. It's not the only component to strengthen organizational culture, but is the easiest to accomplish.

Two key questions are fundamental to creating a culture of hospitality:

1. Is the hospitality guests experience on Sunday morning (or Saturday night) the same as they would experience if they came into the facility at any other time of the week?

2. Is the hospitality in denominational or judicatory offices during the week reflective of the hospitality we expect our churches to exemplify?

The answer to those two questions is critical. To address both in a positive way, it is important to practice both the 5-10-Link and the W.E.A.V.E. in the workplace setting. This doesn't happen by accident or by casual application.

Remember, though, before you *practice* hospitality, you have to determine the organizational cultural value. Simply stated it is this: *The workplace is not the place where we do our job; it is the space where we do our ministry!* Everybody in the workplace—staff and key volunteers—must allow this understanding to become a centerpiece.

Supervisors will need to learn to teach and reinforce this value. The teaching must be regular, consistent, thorough, and engaging. Remember, each new employee or key volunteer will walk into the workplace bringing along her or his own culture. If they are not enculturated into your organization in a healthy way, they will begin to impose their organizational understanding onto yours, leading to a diluted culture and loss of effectiveness. New employees or volunteers aren't doing this because they are saboteurs or mean-spirited; this is just normal human behavior.

For this reason organizations with great culture will spend hours and days embedding their culture into new employees. How much time do you spend teaching your culture to a new employee? Is it intentional? Does it stick? It is obviously important for the church to teach a new employee the necessary set of skills and practices to fulfill his or her job description. But it is perhaps even more important to teach the employee the church's organizational culture. Overlook getting "buy-in" of the culture in a new employee or volunteer at your own peril!

When each employee or key volunteer arrives for work, she or he must totally buy into the idea that when he or she comes on-site or in the field on behalf of the church or organization, he or she is helping produce the ministry. All staff and volunteers must own this cultural understanding that the work environment is not the *place* where they work but the *space* where they do ministry. It is not just a job but also a calling. What happens here is more than just meeting people's needs; it is serving them and the kingdom.

Every bike rider knows it's okay to coast at times. Sometimes coasting is necessary. It allows us to catch our breath and replenish our strength, enjoy our surroundings, rejuvenate our stamina, and set a healthy pace.

But if we coast too long, it is probably because we're going downhill! And the reality is that churches (and denominations) that seem to be going downhill are frequently coasting when it comes to hospitality in the workplace. They simply are not putting in the necessary effort and intention to create a healthy culture that is truly relational, interactive, engaging, and connecting.

Leadership must relentlessly teach people in the workplace to be ambassadors of the culture of the organization because whether workers and volunteers know it or not, they are! In the halls of the workplace, employees and volunteers are constantly teaching those who walk through the door what the culture of the organization is. They might as well be clear, constant, and committed to teaching it well through modeling behavior.

Astonishingly, I have been in way too many denominational offices to do work and have had people walk right past me in the hallway, never smiling, never saying a word, never acknowledging my presence. Sound familiar? It is the same complaint we repeatedly hear from guests exploring a church for the first time.

Imagine you are a preacher serving in a local church. You come into your denominational office for some reason or other, and you experience a complete lack of hospitality. But since this is the culture in the head office, you subconsciously begin to think it is acceptable, or even expected. That's the attitude you take back to the local church, and inadvertently teach your congregation.

Everyone in the workplace should model behavior Monday through Friday that they want the congregation members to demonstrate on Sundays. The wider the gap between the workplace and the sanctuary space, the larger the hole in the hospitality of the organization and the more diluted the culture.

Let's look at some scenarios of introduction in a work environment, where you are likely to meet many strangers as well as those known throughout the organization. Your attitude toward them should be the same: welcoming, friendly, uplifting, contagious. If you treat everyone who walks through the doors as an honored guest—and not a visitor—it can be!

Scenario #11

You and a coworker in the denominational office are holding an impromptu hallway conversation. You are rushed by a deadline and are understandably busy. In walks a layperson from an affiliated local church, heading to the receptionist. Do you let this person walk right by you? Or do you practice the 5-10-Link?

"Good afternoon. How was traffic driving in?" you cheerfully inquire as you approach her, extending your hand. "I'm Jim. I work in the accounting office."

"Never been here before," she offers, "so I'm just thankful I could find the place." And returning your handshake, she continues, "I'm Charlene."

What next? Right! Immediately, you want to make a connection with your coworker.

"Charlene, have you met Philip? He's the guy who keeps all of us in line here when it comes to our budgets. And believe me: he's the kind of guy who helps make all our good ministries happen here in fine fashion!" (*Remember that many people feel beat up by life in many ways throughout the week. Good hospitality builds them up. We create the culture when we consistently refer to our coworkers in glowing, affirming, building-up terms; the behavior will soon become contagious, and those who hear it will begin to emulate it and to talk about others in their church in the same manner. We set the culture.*)

Charlene engages in brief conversation. You find out what she needs and to which office she is going, and one of you escorts her there.

Wherever Charlene goes for the next few weeks in church-related settings, she will brag about her experience at the denominational office. And the more she brags about it back at her local church, the better people there will feel about the home office. Plus, the more she brags about her experience, the more she will internalize it and intuitively seek to replicate it herself back in the hallways of her church!

But in a different version of this scenario, what if the two coworkers, not wanting to be bothered, keep talking while Charlene walks by in the denominational office? Charlene will similarly remember the experience, but as a bad one. Wherever she goes in church settings, she'll talk about how unfriendly the home office is, creating a bad feel in the church toward the denomination. The more she talks about it, the more she will internalize it and begin to exemplify similar behaviors in the hallway of her local church when an inquisitive guest walks down the hallway.

Scenario #12

What if the person walking in the door is the FedEx delivery person? Treat him or her the same way! As you will learn later in the section 2 of this book, everyone who enters your work environment for any reason can be turned into an evangelist for your organization through the power of recommendation. When the FedEx employee leaves your place, you want her or him to be recommending you and your denomination and your churches to others he or she meets in the course of the daily workweek.

"Wow, those folks over there at the Methodist building are great folks," Derek the delivery person might say at his next stop. After a while, little by little, your organization develops the reputation you want it to have. And one day, quite beyond our planning or understanding, the receptionist at the nearby auto dealership, struggling to rebound from an ugly divorce and feeling all alone, will greet Derek the friendly FedEx guy and engage in routine small talk. Wouldn't it be great if in their forty seconds of conversation she heard him recount from his earlier stop, "What great folks they are over in that Methodist center"? Those words, echoing in her mind all weekend, may surface on Sunday morning, and she'll drag herself out of the house to attend for the first time the local United Methodist church. And a life can be changed.

Nonverbal Messaging in the Workplace

So far, we have spoken a lot about messaging: how we introduce ourselves, how we make connections, and how we recommend the church to others. We have stressed that what happens on Sunday morning really has its origins in the culture of the organization, be it a local church or a denominational headquarters.

Our discussion wouldn't be complete without a little focus on the nonverbal messaging as it relates to hospitality in the workplace. We must consider how our work environment (hallways, landscaping, offices, gathering places, etc.) conveys the culture of the organization. (This is discussed more in depth in our book *Creating Culture*.)

Sitting on the plane, reading the in-flight magazine, I (Jim) see more than just information about the plane, the flight, or the airline. Oh, there's some in there. But most of the magazine is about the destinations: the places, things to do, and interesting stories about interesting places and aspects of daily living. There's always a connection between how the airline can get you to those places where you can do those things, but the magazine editors have learned that it's good to focus on other things than themselves.

"It's not about us," is what our culture should shout, rather than, "It's all about us!" In your work environment you can and should have a lot of institutional stuff on the walls, coffee tables, and so on.

But if that is all there is, it quickly, irritatingly communicates that our actions are about us, and not about others!

In the workplace, be sure to display items (what social scientists call "artifacts") from the mission field that match the interests of your target audience. These could include pictures of people and places, maps, displays, and memorabilia. This will demonstrate (and model), "We are not all about ourselves; we are about what *you* are about! We understand you; we get you and want to learn more about your world." If every magazine on the credenza is a churchy magazine, we inadvertently tell our preachers and laity who visit the office that our target audience is churchy people. Is it? If we say we are interested in unchurched, de-churched, disconnected people, why not display magazines and other artifacts that speak to that culture? This communicates our interest in learning about that culture. Take care not to paint a picture that says the church world is solely what we are about and all that we know.

If in denominational offices we convey an "all about us" culture, our churches will begin to pick up that message, and the institutional DNA will go throughout the denomination.

Discussion Questions

1. Can you think of some local businesses with great reputations?

   a. What are they known for specifically?

   b. Are you aware of this business from firsthand experience, or word of mouth?

2. Can you think of one or more local churches with great reputations?

   a. What are they known for specifically?

b. Are you aware of this church through firsthand experience, or word of mouth?

3. Does your church have a reputation for anything in particular?

   a. For what specifically?

   b. How do you know?

4. How do the ministries in your church go about growing their teams—that is, attracting new people?

5. Which of the W.E.A.V.E. elements are strengths of your people? Which are weaknesses?

Chapter 6

Hospitality in the Worship Service

Whenever I see an adult on a bicycle
I have hope for the human race.

—*H. G. Wells*

Bears weren't his only worry, or even his main one. Hypothermia was. Dressed in only a T-shirt, shorts, and sneakers, my (Jim's) son Adam pulled his Jeep Cherokee to the side of the road and let the dogs out to stretch their legs. At this brief stop he wouldn't even unstrap his mountain bike from the back, as he had been doing throughout the day to ride while the dogs jogged along beside him.

Gusting winds whipped the trees but could not deter the blue heeler or the terrier sprinting down a rugged path. Adam let them run. It was only going to be short walk down to what appeared to be a trickling stream and then back to the jeep. He positioned his back-pack, filled with hardcover textbooks on environmental sustainability

81

that he was determined to study in some pleasant meadow while the dogs played.

But they found no meadow. Even for an experienced hiker, it is easy to get lost in the back ridges of the Rockies. A sprinting squirrel provided the first of a few distractions; curiosity to see what lay ahead and the need to avoid a grazing black bear conspired to get them turned around, losing their orientation. Confidence soon shifted to anxiety at the possibility of getting lost. And before long, Adam had to own up that he had no idea where he was, what he should do, or how to get out of the mess.

After four and half hours of walking, anxiety grew faster than their hunger. An experienced hiker, Adam held panic at bay, but nothing could hold off the creeping darkness and dropping temperatures. Or the thirst. The pleasant afternoon had long ago given way to howling winds and darkening skies.

Looking for any guidance, Adam decided to turn it over to the dogs as they began sniffing the air, stubbornly leading Adam in a diagonal direction. Fortunately, as it turned out, toward water. A small, high-altitude lake appeared. At the water's edge Adam could see the snaking red of a mountain road across a jagged ravine. Scrambling toward it, Adam breathed his first sigh of relief in a long time. A road would lead to somewhere. He felt better.

As good luck would have it, within a few minutes a vintage pickup truck rumbled up the mountain road. Two men, squished into the small truck maxed out with gear and supplies, saw him and stopped. Adam explained his plight. The sympathetic men dug out bottles of an energy drink and dried snacks. They even offered to unload their gear and provide a ride, but Adam did not want to put them out any more. Surely the jeep was nearby, he demurred.

The driver surmised that this was the only road up here, but volunteered that they had not seen his jeep up to this point, so, "It must be on up ahead," the driver concluded.

"Be glad to scout for it on our way up to camp," he cheerily offered. Such interchanges happen frequently between truckers and hikers in the back mountain roads, where rugged hospitality often goes hand in hand with survival.

The truck drove off, leaving Adam and his dogs to follow in the same direction. A while later the truck returned. "We saw your jeep about a mile or two up." Everyone agreed a good, brisk hike could get them there before dark and ahead of the brewing storm. When he learned that Adam's heavy, bulky backpack contained nothing helpful for survival, the guy riding shotgun was thoughtful enough to relieve him of that burden. "I'll drop it off at the jeep," he said.

Tired but buoyed by the lowering anxiety level and increased comfort, Adam confidently set out, encouraging the straggling dogs. But soon, panic struck. Up ahead Adam could see that the road split, forming a clearly delineated Y, one branch angling upward, the other more of a straight line across the mountainside. All sorts of scenarios flashed through his imagination as he thought about the consequences of taking the wrong branch of the road. They could walk miles before realizing they had guessed wrong! Anxiety overwhelmed him at the impending decision until he walked up to the actual point of the split. Looking down into the dusty grooves, he saw a simple, large message scratched with a stick into the dirt surface of the road. The message brought him hope and encouragement: "Jeep" (with an arrow pointing the way).

Hospitality is going out of the way to point the way. It is going beyond what is expected simply to help. It is being creative and proactive in answering anticipated questions. It is caring about and going out of your way to make life a little easier for people you may never see again. We practice hospitality in the controlled environment of the church so that we'll become adept at doing it in other, less familiar places, including the mission field, service opportunities, and other unpredictable settings and circumstances.

Most folks who come to our churches for the first time aren't in the same precarious plight as my son, but we often fail to appreciate the level of anxiety a first-time guest can bring with him or her to this new, different, and often strange experience. His or her questions may range from simply, "Where is the children's area?" or "Where are the restrooms?" to much deeper questions about which direction to go at some critical juncture in his or her life.

Remember that often people looking for a church are doing so because they are weighed down by unimaginable burdens. They are sometimes lost in a life decision or circumstance. Frequently life has dealt some blow that has disoriented them or caused them to question their self-confidence.

The goal of hospitality is not to get return customers—that's its by-product. The goal is to reflect the welcoming, caring, loving presence of Jesus Christ. In so doing we help reduce or relieve the anxieties that another person may be feeling. We may become the bridge over which they walk to be introduced to the light of Jesus Christ.

We must always remember that a guest in our church may be walking over that bridge carrying a backpack of concerns heavier than that which my son was shouldering. Whatever we can do to make life (or the guest's experience at our church) easier can become a blessing!

Often people coming to worship for the first time are driven by some life-change issue or personal struggle. How to creatively meet their needs, relieve their anxieties, address their questions, and lighten their burdens is a challenge for any church. And it's also an opportunity.

Creativity brings hospitality to life! Growing up, few things were more fun for me (Jim) than sticking baseball cards to the wheel frame of my bike with a clothespin so the edge of the card clicked against the spokes as the wheels rotated. The faster and louder they were, the better. In my buddies' minds, our rides were transformed from bikes to motorcycles!

It's amazing what a little creativity can do. This chapter is about creative ways to include hospitality in the worship service.

By now, we hope you agree that hospitality is about a genuine enthusiasm toward all who attend. Hospitality is being intentional, relational, interactive, engaging, and connecting. The result is a feel that communicates not only that you are glad guests are present but also that you care about who guests are and what their story is and that you want to be a part of it. We're talking about this happening in an authentic, nonintrusive way, in the gentle spirit of friendship.

So far, we've talked about the individual components of a bicycle and of hospitality. But we all know that there is some indefinable, almost unspeakable feel when enjoying a great bike ride. That same experience is what we are after in worship—a spirit that soars beyond words.

If ushers and greeters and others on hospitality teams can create this type of feel with introductions and connections and engagement, and help it to become the DNA of the entire congregation, then we must also make it the spirit of the worship service! What creates culture in any organization is when there is consistency of messaging throughout the organization. My training partner and co-author, Fiona Haworth, served for several years as director of talent for Southwest Airlines, and she reminds me constantly that a clear and compelling culture is what holds the organization together when it is reflected by each and every employee from the ticket agent in Tulsa to the CEO of the airline.

Culture happens when from top to bottom, throughout every tentacle of the organization, there is clarity and consistency of messaging, behavior, attitude, and actions. It is critical that the spirit of what happens *in* worship, matches what happens *around* worship! Otherwise, you may be doing some good things, but you will hardly be creating a culture of hospitality. The way to create such a culture is to be sure the elements of every worship experience include the five key components of hospitality: intentionality, relationship, interaction, engagement, and connection.

First, make sure that the worship (or at least parts of it) is intentionally interactive and engaging. I don't mean *engaging* in the sense of merely being interesting. Hopefully the message and the entire service will be that! Rather, the service should be engaging in a way that is intentionally interactive with the people who are there.

There's a reason that many companies, like Flixster and Amazon, encourage people to add their own reviews. They have figured out that in today's world people want to be participants and producers, not merely customers and consumers.

Responsive scripture readings, calls to worship, and other litanies served the function of interaction and engagement for generations, and did so well. But these don't function in the same way for many present-day audiences. The culture in which most people live has catapulted interaction and engagement into a whole new sphere, as evidenced by technology, popular television, and entertainment venues. Wherever people go they are enmeshed in a ramped-up world of interaction and engagement. Even the "kiss cam" at professional sporting events isn't designed to be simply entertaining but to interact with the crowd.

In 2013, I (Fiona) was asked by our pastor to chair the stewardship committee, and immediately I thought there must have been a dreadful mistake. Our dear pastor must have had me confused with someone else, since surely a worthy stewardship chair would have an astute financial mind and at least be handy with a spreadsheet. As I am bestowed with neither gift, there was an awkward moment. Then our pastor gently explained his view of the role, and my fleeting moment of dread began to change to excitement. Our church is in a fairly solid financial position. Our opportunity was to engage our members in giving joyfully and generously.

As I gathered a small team together, we explored the concept of extending our preexisting culture of hospitality into a culture of giv-ing. We decided to orient our start-up campaign around the scripture "For where your treasure is, there your heart will be also" (Matthew 6:21 NRSV). And that's when the fun began. We shot an over-the-top video featuring the team disclosing their own "treasures," pas-sions ranging from painting through running to fashion (okay, that one was mine). This nutty little video was posted on our church's Facebook page and attracted a ridiculous amount of attention.

Encouraged by the reaction, we staged a presentation *during* worship the following week, inviting our congregation to write down their own treasures on a slip of paper and drop these into huge trea-sure chests stationed in the narthex. We collected the responses and created a digital word cloud (words arranged in a shape or picture), which we unveiled the following Sunday. What a glorious manifesta-tion of everything that we held dear—and such diversity! We saw treasures like fishing, interior design, exercise, motorbikes, computer games, baseball, football . . . My nine-year old son was thrilled to find the name of his favorite app in the picture!

As we honored our treasures, we turned our gaze to where God might be calling us, how we might treasure God above all, and open our hearts to give generously. Our Commitment Sunday was like no other. The altar was festooned with the treasures that we'd named dur-ing our first weeks—pictures of family, sports equipment, vacation catalogs, even a live turtle! This stewardship campaign was a journey of interaction, engagement, connection, discovery, and renewal. It was a journey into culture. Now, I know what you're thinking—*how did the campaign go?* Okay, so we met our financial goal, but more than that, we started a new conversation: We engaged our church members in a wholehearted and lively dialogue about discipleship. And the steward-ship team itself experienced its own shift in perspective. We knew some of the ideas were risky (the word "crazy" was used more than once), but we leaned into the risk. During our debrief, we talked honestly about what we had learned about overcoming our own resistance to connect with our church members and guests in a new way.

It has taken a while for the church to get beyond simply rolling out our older methods of interaction and engagement in worship. If your church is not intentional about keeping up (in ways that are authentic and mirror your traditions, vision, and values), other churches will quickly fill the vacuum, and younger generations will flock there. We have to realize that the level and intensity of interaction and engagement in all other aspects of modern culture has so accelerated that when the church trots out methods from the 1950s and '60s, they simply do not connect. Such efforts are often perceived not as "old-school" or even irrelevant but more like a foreign language that guests will not likely decipher, nor will they take the time to figure out.

It will be increasingly difficult to speak the language of today's emerging generations in worship if we aren't intentional about finding creative ways for people to be actively engaged. This engagement may be a special feature of the service, the ongoing use of Twitter or texting, or a style of communicating. However your church figures out how to engage with and connect with its target audience, it must match the culture of hospitality you are hoping to create.

If nothing else, try having the final slide on your screens at the conclusion of the worship time read: "If you have questions about anything you heard or experienced today, text #_____ and one of our staff will get back to you within two hours." If you don't use screens, print the message in your bulletin. Be sure that you have a dedicated cell phone that can be rotated among staff or key laity to field any inquiries, and be diligent to provide immediate response.

This simple message tells attenders—especially those in the eighteen-to-thirty-five-year-old range—that you speak their language: thumb! Even if you never get a texted question, you are communicating your desired culture of a connecting, engaging, "it's about you" experience.

When someone does text a question or comment, your response may open the way for greater connection or conversation that may well lead to a church relationship or even a personal friendship.

As a bonus, you've gotten a cell phone number! Keep a database of all cell numbers, and when you are publicizing events—especially hands-on, serving opportunities—send out "blast texts" to all the numbers. This can prove to be a quick and easy way to communicate in relevant fashion with many people who will never read the church paper or other written appeals.

We discussed previously the phenomenon that culture travels on words. Be sure that the words you use from the platform, and that appear on screens and bulletins or worship guides, are carefully thought out with intentionality to connect and create culture. Avoid distancing words that create an unintended chasm between the already connected and the not yet connected. Avoid things like "join us for _____." Instead, focus on the benefits available to anyone who participates in that event. "Join us" shouts two words that can create suspicion in the minds of critical first-time attenders. They aren't ready to "join" anything, and they certainly do not want to be considered fresh meat the church is trying to recruit for its purposes. "Us" further distances guests. They are not part of the "us"—will they be valued if they don't become so? Is the agenda to help them, meet their needs, serve them, engage them, and provide them outlets to serve, or is the agenda to get them to become part of "us"? "Join us" sounds like, "It's all about us!" This language is more "institution" oriented and is less about meeing people where they are. It's just not as pleasant to the person who is not already or at least not particularly inclined to want to become part of the "us." He or she may be attending for the first time simply out of some personal need he or she hopes gets addressed.

We must also actively engage people in ways to become producers of the ministry. It's okay to create expectations: "If you are a first-time guest, you are probably here not just to hear what we have to say but also to find a place and way to make a difference. I invite you to check out how you can do something really helpful at the Habitat House we are working on or in collecting food for the hungry." This helps first-timers see immediate ways to connect with a cause or a purpose. More importantly, they see that your deepest desire for them to connect is more meaningful than institutional—it is missional!

Be intentional, relational, interactive, engaging, and invitational in getting people connected and involved.

Work at ways to deliver content in sermons and messages to which a first-time attender can relate and respond. As a rule of thumb, ask yourself if people will be able to use on Monday what they heard on Sunday. Get beyond the stereotypical understanding of preaching in which you as the preacher are the producer and they as the listeners are consumers. Look for ways to make messages more than just informational or inspirational; make them engaging and interactive. Provide specifics of how people can put into practice what you are talking about, and share real-life stories of people actually doing it!

Actively engage the congregation in sermon planning. Strategically select topics far in advance, and publicize them. Solicit stories via e-mails, texts, Facebook, and so forth that you may want to use in your message. Let people know that their stories may help shape someone else's story. This is relational. It is hospitable. It's engaging. It's connecting. And it's friendly.

The pastor of a struggling church I work with in Florida decided to put this principle into practice. He and his worship team developed a sermon series called "Toxic Relationships." He promoted the series months in advance and solicited real-life stories from people about relationships gone bad. He used some of these stories in his series, but he responded to everyone who shared, thereby strengthening relationships. In addition to focusing on sermons, the team lined up speakers and special programs designed to help people with all sorts of toxic relationships. Attendance during the series skyrocketed, but the lasting impact was the culture it began to create within the church by valuing story, relationship, creativity, and intentionality. Today, that church has moved beyond crisis mode and is growing in health and vitality.

Model a spirit of camaraderie, teamwork, and fun on the platform! What happens when a first-time guest sees and experiences elaborate hospitality with great buzz and laugher and an effervescent spirit when he or she walks in? That guest feels connected! Now imagine what happens when what that same guest sees and experiences during the worship service is rote, staid, and mechanical, even if it is done with great dignity and efficiency. Even when all the individual parts of the service are done well, if the feel does not match the feel of the hospitality the guest has experienced in the hallway, there is a disconnect!

This type of disconnect makes it difficult for first-time guests to navigate smoothly through the experience we want them to have. Faster-growing churches have grasped the importance of matching the hospitality *around* the worship service with the hospitality *in* the worship service. That is a key to creating a *culture* of hospitality.

Creating a culture of hospitality is as easy as riding a bike! The variety of bicycles is fascinating. Want to ride a mountain bike? Or a street bike? Or a three-speed or a ten-speed racing bike? You have to determine what you want to do, what you want to accomplish, and what you want the culture to look like. Then select the bike that fits what you want to accomplish. In the church world, you as leader must decide what kind of bike you want to ride and then be sure you are doing ministry the way that matches the bike. There is no single way to do this. There are many avenues to creating a hospitable culture, just as there are many varieties of bicycles.

Discussion Questions

1. What would a first-time guest experience at your church on a typical Wednesday morning?

2. Does your workspace represent you?

3. Describe a time when you experienced great hospitality where you work or at some other business venue.

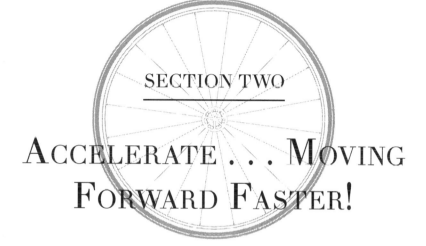

SECTION TWO

ACCELERATE . . . MOVING FORWARD FASTER!

Chapter 7

Shifting Gears: Leveraging a Culture of Hospitality into Growth

On riding a bike: "It never gets easier, you just go faster."
—*Leo Tolstoy*

The "Hotter n' Hell 100" in Wichita Falls, Texas, is one of the state's premier bicycling events. Set in grueling Northwest Texas terrain in sweltering heat, the race attracts thousands of riders. Burt Palmer, pastor of Polk Street UMC in Amarillo, rides in it annually. Like most expert riders, he eagerly talks about his sport. Here is an early exchange that I (Jim) had with Burt:

"I clip in," explained Burt, "because I have to if I want to be successful and survive the conditions." He added, "Most people think that when you ride, you get your forward thrust from the downstroke, when you are pushing the pedals downward. But experienced riders know you add to your thrust with the upswing, when you rotate the pedals back up! That's why you have to clip in—which means you actually lock the bottom of your cycling shoe into the pedal, so your foot can effortlessly pull the pedal back up. That's how you increase your speed while decreasing your energy expended. And believe me, brother: at 265 pounds, I want to make sure every bit of energy I expend helps me get up the hill!"

"But," I continued in my questioning, "isn't that dangerous to have your foot attached to the pedal? What if you crash and can't free yourself from the bike?"

"Sure, there's a risk," answered Burt, "but the risk is well worth it! At the bottom of my cycling shoe is a cleat that is adjustable, so I also can make sure that the alignment of my knee is directly over the ball of my foot; this maximizes my efficiency in effort as well. When I slow down and get ready to stop, I gently twist my ankle out to free my cycling shoe from the pedal. A cyclist who hasn't mastered unclipping might lose control and start to swerve, maybe even take a pretty hard fall. But cyclists manage this risk for the greater reward of increased speed, greater endurance, and energy efficiency."

There's something about riding a bicycle that draws out from the rider the innate desire to move forward faster! Wasn't it like that for you when you were learning? Maybe you wanted to keep up with the bigger kids or your older brother or sister, maybe you enjoyed the thrill of going fast, or maybe you wanted to show off or simply get somewhere quicker. For whatever reason, riding a bike took speed to a whole new level. Beyond keeping our balance to stay up, we intuitively want to accelerate—to go faster!

In addition to clipping in, every rider knows there are several ways to speed up. Going down a steep hill is the easiest, and a favorite, way to speed up for young cyclers. But we quickly learn that sooner or later we've got to pump back uphill, which is the plight of many older churches today.

There's the eternally optimistic hope of having the wind always at your back. Sounds good, but it just doesn't happen that way, at least not in the church world since maybe the 1950s. In today's religious climate we face stiff headwinds seemingly at every turn.

Of course there is the urge to pedal faster and pump harder, which is what most of our churches are trying to do. We go to great expense to retrain congregants, reequip clergy, and rethink church. Denominations and churches alike are trying to get clearer about fruitfulness, results, and accountability. Sadly, most of the time the "pedal faster and pump harder" approach is the fearful reaction to the reality of institutional desperation and decline. Frequently that's the way local church pastors perceive it when the system is mandating its latest attempt at accountability and push for fruitfulness.

Church and denominational leaders have learned the basic truth of bicycling: The slower you go, the more you wobble; the more you wobble, the slower you go. If you go too slowly, you tip over and fall down. You stop. There is nothing wrong with pedaling faster and pumping harder. Most advanced riders train and practice for this necessity and clip in to capitalize on their efforts. But often—especially when riders don't see the fruit of their efforts   the result is frustration and fatigue, another reality of many mainline churches today.

This section champions a different approach: shifting gears. Like the rider of the ten-speed street bike, we still have to put a lot of effort and work into it, but we can leverage our energy and efforts to get better results. You'll learn here how to leverage the key components of a culture of hospitality—intentionality, relationship, interaction, engagement, connection—into accelerating church growth faster.

Recall that in section 1 we stressed that genuine hospitality has no goal of getting anything in return—even getting people to return. In this section we shift gears, exploring how to leverage the key components of hospitality *in other ways* to grow the church faster. You are going to learn new ways to use the two gears that propel a church forward faster:

1. Recommendation: Why it gets more traction than invitation

2. Connection: Getting people involved faster, which closes the consumer/producer gap

While the above two items are not expressly hospitality, they catapult up from hospitality. They will not be possible without having first created a culture of hospitality. When appropriately practiced (and you'll learn step-by-step how to do in the next two chapters), a first-time attender can speedily and steadily move from being a consumer of what the church has to provide to becoming a producer of what the church provides.

If this book is achieving its goal, you are seeing how hospitality can be correlated to the process of learning to ride a bike. First, you gain balance and momentum through creating a culture of hospitality. Second, you use that balance and momentum to accelerate your church's growth. And third, as we'll discuss in the epilogue, you work on endurance—the last essential ingredient of good bike riding, the lasting impression of culture.

In the brilliant business book *Change the Culture, Change the Game,* authors Roger Connors and Tom Smith rightly point out two truths that are applicable to our work in the church world:

1. The results you are getting are because of the culture you have; if you want to change the results, you have to change the culture.

2. Most organizations grow by *reaching* people, getting people to *return*, and getting returners to *recommend* to others (the three R's).

In order to create a strong culture—such as a culture of hospitality—we must change the results we've been getting in our local churches and denomination, and learn to accelerate our growth by accomplishing the three R's. Our experience is that churches grow at the pace with which the three R's occur:

1. Reaching

2. Returning

3. Recommending

The Participant Pyramid

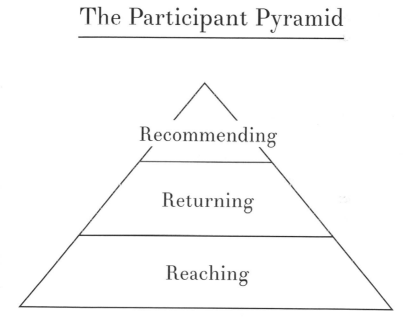

The Participant Pyramid

A focus on the three R's will drive churches to reach new participants, get them to return, and then motivate them to recommend the church to others. Like other organizations that depend on new clientele or participants, churches must structurally be designed and oriented to excel at all three. I went into the ministry under the amazing missionary and evangelist E. Stanly Jones. He used to say that "the church is not an organization . . . it is a living organism." While I agree with the sentiment behind the statement, it is not totally accurate. Too much organization can stifle the energy of the living organism. But too little or ineffective organization can choke the growth of the living organism by turning its activities and movement into a chaotic mess. The church is both a living organism and an organization. If it is to "prevail against the gates of hell," it has to incorporate both understandings and excel at each. It is the organizational culture of the church that allows it to excel at the three R's.

Reaching. Often, reaching new people is actually easy for a church but leads to only the lowest tier of growth. Many churches are excited about getting to this tier and then stop or coast to a standstill; their growth ceases and they simply spin their wheels without going forward. Denominations and church-planting movements have figured out that the best way to reach new people is to start new churches. Similarly, within an existing church the best way to reach new people is to start a new ministry (worship service, hands-on helping initiative, new staff member, etc.). There is something about newness that provides a good opportunity to reach people who previously were not connected to the church, or perhaps any church, or even to the gospel. But as Jim Griffith and Bill Easum point out, even new churches can quickly lost their evangelistic zeal to reach new people without constant attention to staying outwardly focused (*Ten Most Common Mistakes Made by New Church Starts* [St. Louis: Chalice Press, 2008]).

But new isn't always necessary. Many churches have experienced a jump-start in numbers by having special events like Christmas Eve, Easter, or Mother's Day services that they promote heavily in the community with top-notch media blitzes. Or sometimes a church will find itself the beneficiary of a new housing development nearby. With just a little prompting, the youth group or some other group of church parishioners can distribute doorknob hangers and may actually see results the coming Sunday. In this case, it isn't the church that is new but the people who are new! And this is a prime time to reach new people. But reaching people (whatever the number) results only in tier 1 growth. It can actually become counterproductive because sometimes a church attempts repeated efforts to reach new people with little success, demoralizing even their best leaders.

Returning. A church with a good marketing campaign can often reach people, but getting those folks to return requires two things. The first is a good product, which includes a worship experience that is worthy of returning to, an environment that is attractive and inviting and welcoming, a compelling vision, a missional focus, quality child care, a genuine sense of hospitality, and an effective way to connect to people. The second factor necessary for people to return is the success and pace with which you can get the first-time attender to become significantly involved in the ministry of the church, moving from consumer to producer.

The reason getting people involved faster is critical is not so much because of the "thing" or "ministry" they may be doing; rather, it is because of the relationships and friendships that develop during the doing! Imagine immediately after worship, attenders are encouraged to stop for twenty minutes at the back of the sanctuary to assemble sandwiches to take to the nearby homeless shelter. Two new guests who don't even know each other are stationed across from one another, slapping peanut butter and jelly on bread; they smile and talk . . . a relationship develops. That's what grows churches!

Getting to the next tier of growth requires that a significant number of the people you've reached actually return. Given worship attendance trends of late, this return may or may not be the very next Sunday after their initial visit. Oftentimes returns are random and sporadic. But still, getting a sizable number (whatever the number for your context) of people you have reached to return will jump-start the church to second-tier growth.

Don't dismay over current trends in worship attendance, even among regular members. Most of us in the church world grew up in a time when a loyal church member attended every Sunday, or, at worst, three out of four Sundays. Now, most research and anecdotal evidence suggests a loyal member today will attend about 1.2 times a month, as reported in *Get Their Name: Grow Your Church by Building New Relationships* by Bob Farr, Doug Anderson, and Kay Kotan.

Pastors, don't panic! It does not help to berate your congregation on Sunday mornings for more people not being present. Scolding does not go over well, and is offensive to the folks who are, in fact, present. The value of getting people to return is not so much in the number and frequency of return visits, but in the connectional bond they form!

Recommending is where exponential, accelerated growth happens in the life of a local church. Recommending seems simple but like riding a bike takes practice to master. The results can be contagious! Here is a real-life recent conversation with my (Jim's) adult nephew, who told me about the church he and his family are now attending in the Austin area:

Nephew: "We don't go to our old Methodist church anymore. We liked it okay, but we love our new church. Lots of people in our neighborhood go there."

Me: "I'm curious. Why did you go the first time? Did somebody invite you?"

Nephew: "Oh no. We just heard everybody talking about it all the time, so we decided to give it a try."

Notice it wasn't an invitation but a recommendation that resulted in my nephew changing churches. In the next chapter we'll share how you can accelerate your church's growth by teaching people the importance of and the how-tos of recommending the church to their friends, coworkers, and even strangers. We're not trashing invitation, as you will see. Invitation and recommendation are first cousins who love to play together; they have as much fun as riding a "bicycle built for two!"

One last thing about shifting gears: Experienced riders tell me the right time to shift gears is while you are pedaling, not while you are coasting. While it is rotating, the sprocket movement allows the chain to slip onto the new gear more easily. If you try to change gears while you are coasting, you risk the likelihood of having the chain slip off the sprocket.

The best time to shift gears is while you are pedaling forward. So don't think that you will need to stop many or any of your current ministries to implement what we'll be talking about in the final two chapters. Keep pedaling! There's no need to slow down or coast. Just shift gears and you will move forward faster, easier, and longer!

Discussion Questions

1. Think about a recent sermon that you heard. What spoke to you? What was most relevant?

2. Have you ever e-mailed your pastor a topic suggestion for his or her sermon? What was it?

3. What are some pros and cons of "sharing your story" in a way that may be used in your pastor's sermon?

Chapter 8

Why "Recommendation" Gets More Traction than "Invitation"

Life is like a 10-speed bike; most of us have gears we never use.
—Charles Schulz

As a young boy, I (Jim) was in church every Sunday in rural Illinois with my family. I still remember the first joke I heard a preacher tell in a sermon. It was about a cute conversation between an eight-year-old and his mother.

"Johnny," the mother said, "did you remember at school today to invite Suzy to your birthday party?"

"Mom," Johnny answered, disgusted at the thought of his irritating neighbor Suzy coming to his special day, "I not only invited her to come . . . I dared her to!"

The church has been talking about and relying upon invitation since the beginning. But many if not most church folks have developed some kind of protective shield to keep them from actually inviting someone new to come to church with them.

Most of us have our own hesitancies about invitation. The act seems simple, but in truth, it's not. In their book *Get Their Name*, Bob Farr, Doug Anderson, and Kay Kotan develop the metaphor of the public school system—including elementary school, middle school, high school, college, and graduate school—to demonstrate that people in an elementary evangelism posture aren't really equipped for or comfortable with the rather significant stage of inviting. They can still do evangelism at their stage of spiritual growth, but they probably aren't ready to make actual, personal invitations. There are important stage-building steps that can be done in the elementary school stage that will help these individuals grow into middle school and beyond. *Get Their Name* is a helpful book to use in local church study groups. Our book builds on their work by tackling one of the easiest and most important capabilities in the elementary and middle school metaphor (and throughout one's faith journey): recommending the church to others.

We in the church have our own perspective of invitation as a good, albeit underutilized practice. But it's wise to remember that the invitee, especially if she or he is outside the church, sees our invitation with a heavy dose of skepticism. Good church folks are intuitively aware of this resistance, which is one of the barriers to getting people to follow a F.R.A.N. plan (friends, relatives, acquaintances/associates, and neighbors) and actually invite them.

Many folks have received one too many invitations to a dinner event initially described as an opportunity to talk about retirement, and then realized the agenda was to sell financial products. Or they have accepted one too many invitations to coffee with a neighbor, coworker, or friend, and then been pressured to become part of a multilevel marketing scheme.

I (Jim) even responded once to a personal, handwritten invitation to tour a beautiful new housing development on the riverfront with the promise that I would receive a brand-new bass boat just for coming. After all day with a pushy salesman, I finally walked back to the parking lot with my bass boat under my arm. That's right. It was an inflatable bass boat about as useless as the invitation!

In our world today we are not often inviting people with neutral attitudes and opinions about church, people who've been sitting around all day waiting for our invitation. We are often inviting skeptics, or even antagonists who have been subconsciously raised on Mary Howitt's classic poem "The Spider and the Fly." Many of us learned the first verse in elementary school.

> "Will you walk into my parlour?" said the Spider to the Fly;
> "'Tis the prettiest little parlour that ever you did spy;
> The way into my parlor is up a winding stair,
> And I've many curious things to show when you are there,"
> "Oh no, no," said the little Fly, "to ask me is in vain,
> For who goes up your winding stair can ne'er come down
>   again."

While the poem is really a long fable, mostly about vanity and flattery—how the cunning spider used flattery to get the fly into his web—most folks recall only the first verse about invitation (and possible motives behind the invitation). Unconnected people may carry an understandable skepticism of invitations they receive in the mail or from friends who have asked them to join a multilevel scheme or franchising enterprise. They may be wary of the motives surrounding all invitations.

Another underlying assumption of the invitation model is the notion that churched people have a reservoir or network of unchurched people to invite, which is seldom the case. Churches, and especially mainline churches, unintentionally institutionalize adherents into the church world, and out of the mission field. Here is how this happens:

1. A new person actually joins the church! Maybe this person is already churched and has just moved into the area or is unhappy with his or her previous church, but for the sake of our argument here, let's assume this person is a new convert, coming to faith for the first time.

2. To surround him or her with Christian support, we apply subtle pressures to get this person involved and connected (not bad things), helping him or her make friends in a Sunday school class or some other group (again, not bad things).

3. Soon, his or her circle of friends revolves around only people this person has met in the church, or in church activities or parachurch ministries, like Emmaus (not bad things).

4. Gradually, this person is being drawn out of the unchurched network and into the churched network (again, not a bad thing but a process that hampers reaching new people).

5. Slowly the new convert become more and more disconnected from earlier friendships outside the church world. The older the church and the longer a person's tenure in the church, the more ingrained this phenomenon becomes (not a good thing, but most people in a church, especially an older church, think it is a good thing).

6. At some point the church becomes desperate for new life and new people. So in survival mode, the church attempts to motivate, train, and deploy that person *back* into the unchurched mission field. This last step is often so unnatural and contrived, so countercultural to what he or she has been experiencing for so long, that this person resists our efforts to get him or her back into the mission field, and the church

continues its path to decline. During the process churches often circle the wagons and resist attempts to become relevant again, especially since it often involves dramatic, wholesale change.

This scenario is played out in countless churches across the country. So then, when the churched person does invite an unchurched person, it is not really a friend inviting a friend but more likely a churched person inviting a stranger or acquaintance, with little result other than a residue of awkwardness. (The above is a problem discussed, with some solutions offered, in Farr et al., *Get Their Name*).

Another problem inherent in the expectation that church members will become proficient with invitation is what I call the "Dos Equis Effect." Recall those popular commercials in which "the Most Interesting Man in the World" ends the spot by saying, "I don't often drink beer, but when I do, I prefer Dos Equis." Marketers have begun to understand that brand loyalty has changed. "Loyalty" doesn't necessarily mean *always*, but it can mean *preference*. That preference will lead to the consumer recommending the brand to others.

Today's changing attendance patterns don't mean people love the church any less. Family and life schedules have changed, creating newly emerging patterns and trends. But changing attendance patterns add an awkward wrinkle to inviting a friend because it is so much more difficult to coordinate timing—to have the friend's availability match your own availability. Effective churches have learned how to engage people—even their loyal members—in ways outside of regular worship attendance.

What this means in today's church world is that when someone you've reached attends the church for the first time and then returns for a second or third visit (or more, the timing of which may be random and sporadic), he or she will still recommend the church to others. Often he or she will use language similar to that in a Dos Equis advertisement: "We don't get to go as much as we'd like, but when we do go to church, we go to FaithBridge; you'd enjoy checking it out."

People have to say something like that only once or twice before the church to which they return (*at whatever frequency*) will go from being *the* church to *our* church. Amazingly, this loyalty dynamic happens quite fast. As *Change the Culture, Change the Game* shows, when a new person in an organization tells just *one other* person about the good things in that organization, he or she begins to form brand loyalty and become institutionalized into the organization. Similarly, when an attender—longtime or new—recommends the church to just one other person, he or she develops a loyalty to the church! This is a kind of loyalty that, aside from worship attendance patterns, may lead to other connections in terms of financial support, missional involvement, and volunteering to work on specific, short-term needs.

We (Jim and Fiona) attend dozens of worship services in different churches every year. Way too often we hear preachers implore along the scripted lines: "Come back next week, and bring a friend." The preacher boasts a wide smile, thinking, "This is so obvious, so easy. Why don't they just do it?" And the listeners are subconsciously thinking, "Yeah, right." The congregation and preacher engage in one of those ritualistic dances of good intention, little action.

We don't know of reliable studies on this, but just looking at church attendance patterns across the country, it seems very few church folk actually invite someone to church that results in the invitee coming with them. True, when this actually does happen, the invited person has a much higher likelihood of staying and getting connected, so don't stop inviting! But elevate "recommending" to a top priority in your approach.

Today's popular workshops (like Jim Griffith's highly effective "How to Reach New People") are teaching churched people to rediscover ways to network in the mission field with unchurched folks. This is not a natural behavior for most church pastors and people,

109

at least in mainline church traditions. Newer, nondenominational churches seem more hardwired to motivate their active participants to reach back into their sphere of unchurched relationships and invite new guests.

But in mainline traditions, church life itself makes this difficult. Our older, denominational culture tends to draw a person so deeply into the church community (Sunday school classes, activity groups, and so forth) that soon the attender joins, and then surrounds him- or herself with church friends in church settings so much so that that he or she loses track of any unchurched relationships he or she had prior to joining the church.

People who have a hard time inviting might find it much more to their liking to recommend the church to a friend, family member, coworker, neighbor, or acquaintance they've casually met at the gym or some other such setting. The good news is that once people start recommending and experience some success, they may actually move up to inviting.

When someone has had a rich and impactful experience through our church, they cannot help but want to tell others of it! We don't even have to prompt them—it's natural. And it's easier, more comfortable, and more doable than inviting someone to join us the next Sunday. So this is a behavior on which church leaders can learn to capitalize and can leverage for kingdom impact.

Think about it. Most people don't really invite their neighbors to join them at the great new restaurant they discovered last weekend. Schedules are too difficult; family dynamics and lifestyles are too different; timing is too shaky. But most people do eat at that restaurant because someone recommended it.

Which happens more often to you? Do you go to a hot new movie with someone who invites you, or because someone you trust has recommended you see it? If it is more often the latter, you are motivated to see it on your own schedule and when the timing is right, not having the hassle of coordinating with someone else. Sure—invitation does happen, and it is often more fun to go to that movie as an invited guest. But most often, it is recommendation, not invitation, that gets you there.

We are hardwired to recommend! For generations, people looking for a job have been required by employers to secure letters of recommendation. What others say about us adds credibility and trustworthiness. When I (Jim) read my *Men's Health* online magazine, there is always the button to click and read "most recommended" articles. When I (Fiona) look at my Flixster app, there is always the icon to click that says, "Tell a friend."

Craigslist and many other online mediums are built on recommendations.

Put yourself in the shoes of your parishioners, and think about why they may find it awkward to invite someone to church.

1. It might seem easier to invite a friend, family member, or coworker, but it is more awkward to invite someone you've just met in a social gathering or in some civic activity or sporting league. After all, you don't really know him or her. What if that person turns out to be someone you don't really want to form a close friendship with? It makes much more sense simply to say, "We go to Impact Church. It has about everything my family could want." This does not put your new acquaintance on the spot, asking him or her to arrange his or her schedule to coordinate with yours, or seem too pushy.

2. If studies are right, the average loyal attender in worship is only there about 1.2 weeks a month. To invite someone to come with you makes it difficult to coordinate schedules. And awkward. The invitee may be thinking, "You want to invite me the next time you go, which is in three weeks? You must not be too on fire for this church."

3. Many church members may worry the invitee will not have a good experience. After all, people have different tastes in music. A good sermon to one person may seem far from such to another. Some people like big churches; others prefer smaller ones. Or a church member may like his or her church because of friends and history but may not really be sure if it is worthy of inviting someone else to attend! If the person you invite accepts your invitation, he or she might end up riding with you or sharing a meal with you afterward. This can be great, but it can also be awkward if you have to debrief an experience that may not have been all that good for your friend. It's much easier to say, "Hey, if you are looking for a church right now, you might want to check out River of Life. My family and I have really enjoyed it."

I (Jim) am a dad living in Dallas, and at one time I wanted my son, who was living in Colorado and going through a tough time, to find a church in which he could make some connections. I called a pastor colleague in Dallas, and he recommended a pastor and church near my son based on recommendations he had heard from other people. I then called my son and, based on my friend's recommendation, told him about the church. He is now active there. I couldn't invite him to go with me, because we are miles away. And no one from there invited him to attend. It was recommendation.

Please don't misunderstand. We are not advocating that you stop inviting people. Personal invitation is still the best way to grow a church. But the reality is that most people are not comfortable with or accomplished at inviting someone to attend church with them. And most receivers of those invitations are not inclined to accept, for a variety of reasons we've already discussed.

The church has proudly taken steps to move from an attraction model of the '60s to an invitation model. However, the culture we live in has moved more and more to a recommendation model.

Learning to leverage recommendation is a must, if for no other reason than to be culturally relevant to the context in which we live and do ministry!

So while not stopping or diminishing the importance of inviting, our experience is that if we direct more time and attention to teach, encourage, and motivate everyone who comes through our doors, both long timers and newcomers, to recommend our church, we will gain more traction in the mission field. We will explore this further in the next chapter.

Psalm 145:4-12 (NIV) tells of the advantage of recommending (or *commending*, as scripture is sometimes translated): "One generation commends your works to another; *they* tell of your mighty acts. *They* speak of the glorious splendor of your majesty . . . *They* tell of the power of your awesome works . . . *They* celebrate your abundant goodness . . . *They* tell of the glory of your kingdom and speak of your might" (emphasis ours). When we can get one generation (or one person) to recommend our church to another generation (or someone else), *they* will tell of it in splendid, convincing ways that elicit a response!

Mother's Day was coming up, and I (Jim) wandered the mall, looking for the perfect gift. I was intrigued by the stand set up in the hallway with a sign reading: Name Rings.

"Buy a ring and put the names of your children on it; your wife will love it!" coaxed the young man operating the kiosk. I looked but was still uncertain. He tried everything. "I'll cut you a deal." "Look. See how lovely the ring is." "How many children do you have?" "Four?" "I'll put the fourth name on for free."

I wasn't moved until a woman walked by, pushing a stroller and holding the hand of her older daughter. Overhearing our conversation, the woman stopped, showed me her ring, and said, "I love this thing! My husband got it for me last year, and it is my favorite gift! Your wife would love it!"

So I bought one! Not because of the dealer's coaxing and inviting but because of the recommendation of a satisfied, happy customer who had become an evangelist for the product.

This is the dynamic that grows churches. Develop a church culture where on-fire members are so excited they can't wait to recommend the church to others! Sounds too good to be true, doesn't it? That's because it's our fantasy church! The reality is that pastors and leadership have to do the hard work of teaching our people why and how to recommend.

Discussion Questions

1. Are you comfortable asking someone to visit your church?

2. What are some ways that you have invited someone to attend your church?

3. What motivated you to first check out the church you attend now?

4. Why did you return?

Chapter 9

Turning "Attenders" into "Recommenders"

When I was a kid I used to pray every night for a new bicycle.
Then I realized that the Lord doesn't work that way so
I stole one and asked Him to forgive me.

—*Emo Philips*

Grandfather Mountain is one of the most popular tourist spots in America. Boasting scenic views and interpretive history of the geography and wildlife of the Blue Ridge Mountains, this drive-through national treasure features a mile-high swinging bridge. Located in the high country of North Carolina, the park receives millions of visitors annually, whom the staff treat as guests. A good visit will be an investment of two to six hours, depending on how long you enjoy the wildlife areas and explore the multitude of hiking trails.

The entry fee pays some salaries, and I (Jim) suppose someone is making a profit somewhere, but the Grandfather Mountain

Stewardship Foundation (which owns and operates the experience and which provides an excellent self-guided interpretive tour CD to play as you drive along) has a purpose and mission: to educate the public and preserve the natural wonder of the area.

Here's the teachable moment for the church. As you descend down the mountain, right at the exit is a big sign reading:

WE HOPE YOU WILL TELL YOUR FRIENDS
YOU ENJOYED GRANDFATHER MOUNTAIN.

The good folks who run this mountain adventure have discovered the power of recommendation! And the church can do the same.

Notice the sign doesn't read: "Thanks for coming! We hope you had a good time and will come again." There's nothing wrong with that sentiment and courtesy, but it simply asks people if they had a good consumer experience and will come to consume again. The sign doesn't read: "We hope you had a good time; come again and bring a friend." Again, there's nothing wrong with that sentiment, but it asks people to do something that feels awkward, and so they are not likely to do it. "If I invite a neighbor to come with me, does that mean I'll pay his or her entry fee?" "When can we get our schedules coordinated?" "What if they don't like hairpin curves like I do?" And on and on.

Expressly asking me (Jim) to "tell my friends" (recommend), transfers my good experience as a *consumer* of the product of the Grandfather Mountain experience into a *producer* for the Grandfather Mountain experience! Amazingly, I have to recommend the experience to only one or two people, and I begin to feel an allegiance to the mountain, as though I have something at stake in its purpose and mission. I feel good about my recommending, and the more I recommend, the better I feel about Grandfather Mountain. If they can turn me from a consumer into a producer, it is a win-win for everybody. Same for the church.

When we decide we want to change not only the results we have been getting but also our culture as a whole, then we can come up with creative ways to reach our desired outcome of growing. The fastest way to grow is to get people who attend to recommend. Whether attenders are longtime loyal members, sporadic in their pattern of attendance, or first-time guests, they all can be motivated to recommend the church to someone else.

Much is said today of the adaptive challenge or change—change that goes beyond the technical change, into the deeper, substantive change. This is the kind of change that comes from asking new and difficult questions, and that often results in opening up new understandings of reality.

Adaptive change is much like the 1860s introduction of the "girls' bike," with its unique frame that allowed women to wear long dresses and skirts in keeping with the fashion of the day. This wasn't just a technical design style; it was an adaptive change that opened people's minds—mainly men's minds—about the function and purpose of the bicycle. The church must likewise be involved in such adaptive change. One change that seems to have completely eluded the mainline church is the change from maintaining a limited understanding of a culture of invitation (helpful in previous generations) to utilizing the role of recommendation while building up to invitation.

When we talk about a culture of invitation, we are really talking about rethinking recommendation. As your members grow in their discipleship path, they become more open to, skilled in, and adept at inviting. But along the way on their journey, they can easily learn to recommend. Before we can get to a culture of invitation, we must master the art of recommendation.

When we expect people to invite, we are generating an evangelism expectation suitable for accomplished and adept riders, but we are often talking to people still on training wheels or at least wobbly on the two-wheeled bike. To expect a novice to be able to accomplish the feat of a rider who is skilled enough and far enough along in the discipleship process to pop a wheelie or ride no-handed, is probably not well thought out.

Recommendation is the easiest, lightest form of evangelism. People can be brand-new to the church and still sense the need and seize the opportunity to recommend well before they get to the higher level of inviting. Nothing is wrong with invitation; it's agreed that it is the best form of church growth, and a behavior to which all our members should aspire. But we leave too much on the table if we wait for people to mature in their faith journey until they feel comfortable and adept enough to invite. And we are often setting ourselves up for frustration if we expect them to invite before they have moved far into their faith journey and loyalty to the church.

Consider this chart relating the significant stages of spiritual growth to the various stages of recommendation.

Four Phases of Recommendation

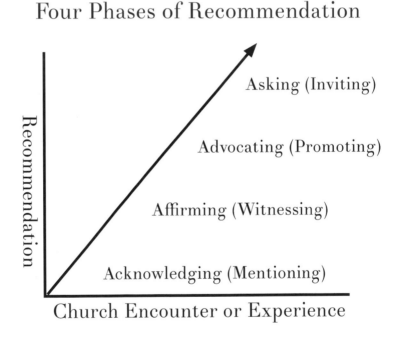

Asking (Inviting)

Advocating (Promoting)

Affirming (Witnessing)

Acknowledging (Mentioning)

Church Encounter or Experience

Note—This chart is not designed for church leaders to monitor the effectiveness of their members in these areas. It is designed for church leaders to assess their effectiveness in teaching and motivating members/attenders to recommend.

Acknowledging: This is the entry phase of recommendation and includes behavioral examples such as the following: (1) Checking in on Facebook during worship service (hopefully at the urging of the worship leader) or "liking" the church's website. (2) Mentioning the church's name in conversation outside the church, for instance, with a coworker at the office: "That's cool that the sales division of our company is going to Habitat this Saturday; Lakewood Church—where I go—does that, too!" (3) Specifically referencing an attribute of the church to a target audience or in social media. For instance, circulating a notice where you work: "First Church Grand Prairie is collecting canned goods for the hungry this Thanksgiving. If you'd like to help, let me know and I'll pick them up."

Affirming: This second phase of recommendation is characterized by more strategic, specific focus. Behavioral examples include: (1) Checking in on Facebook with a comment such as, "Enjoying great music at Shepherd's Community UMC this morning!" (2) Purposely being more pointed in a workplace conversation or in a Twitter feed: "Loved going to Living Faith church last week; message really spoke to me!" (3) Allowing a fifteen-second video of your personal story of the church's impact in your life to be shared on screens during morning worship: "I work with Joel Phillips. When he recommended my family try out Falls Chapel, we decided to. I'm so glad we did; my kids have never been happier in church."

Advocating: This is the third phase of recommending, in which people become more intentional and proactive, putting their own judgment and reputations on the line. Behavioral examples might include: (1) Forwarding to folks on your contact list a creative, compelling electronic flyer (sent by the church) promoting an upcoming sermon series; with the forward you include a *personal comment*: "Hey, check out this sermon series—'Just Married.' This church has really helped strengthen our marriage." (2) Being intentionally self-revelatory in talking to another person who may be going through

119

some tough challenge: "The support group at Living Faith church really helped me when we were going through tough times with our teenager; I think it would help you, too." (3) In the terminology of the United Methodist membership vows, *witnessing*, or sharing how the church has impacted you: "I've been a skeptic of church for a long time, but I've learned a lot here."

Asking: This is the inviting phase and the highest form of recommendation. Behavioral examples might include: (1) Posting on your Facebook page a picture of Connections UMC with worship times listed or information on some special event, like a concert: "I'll be here for the July 4 Patriotic Extravaganza. Want to join me?" (2) Inviting someone with whom you have a relationship to join you for church: "We love our church! Why don't you come with us? We'd love to pick you up or have lunch together afterward." (3) "I know you are the kind of guy who loves to build things. We could sure use your help on our Habitat House. How 'bout it? Can you join us next Saturday morning?"

Invitation is the highest form of recommendation. The church world has long known that the driver that leads to growth is personal invitation. Often what leads to exponential growth in today's world is recommendation!

Recommendation may come easier than invitation, but let's be honest in recognizing that it is not perfect or ideal. Many people have some old messages playing in their heads about recommendation. It could be the principal pointing a finger and growling, "I recommend you straighten up and fly right, buster!" Or we remember mom, frustrated and scolding, "I recommend you get this mess cleaned up before your father gets home!" Recommending can have a heavy-handedness to it, a coercive directive hidden within. We want to be careful how we use the word *recommendation*.

And we want to remember that the whole point of recommendation (and ultimately of invitation) is to move people lovingly into the community of faith called the church. Truth is, identification is the purest form of recommendation. We aim to live our lives so that people identify us as Christ followers, as participants in our church. "They'll know we are Christians by our love," declares the song. As scripture says, "Be imitators of God" (Ephesians 5:1 NASB). Ideally, when we are immediately, clearly, and convincingly identified with the body of Christ, that is the best recommendation! Jesus was big on this. So was Paul.

In the New Testament, the apostle Paul identifies the best way to recommend: "Are we beginning to commend ourselves again? Or do we need, like some people, letters of recommendation to you or from you? You yourselves are our letter, written on our hearts, known and read by everyone" (2 Corinthians 3:1-2 NIV).

We want people to recommend because they are motivated out of their own personal witness to the gospel's life-changing power. Said Jesus, "Go and tell John what you hear and see" (Matthew 11:4 NRSV).

How we, as followers of the risen Christ and participants in the community of faith called the church, actually live out our faith is the best way to recommend it to others! The next best way is to teach congregants how to recommend the church and to reinforce their behavior when they make the effort to do so.

Three Simple Ways to Create a Culture of Recommendation

First: "Trustimonials" (a version of testimonials that feature people whom others trust or can relate to). With today's technology, you can have a talking head video trustimonial from someone's cell phone in a matter of minutes. Be on the lookout for good stories! When you hear someone (or of someone) who says something like,

"We came this morning because the Jenkinses recommended we try the church," simply ask him or her to say it again on a cell phone video. I (Jim) have done this hundreds of times in churches across the country, and I never had anyone say no to my request. Most everyone is delighted, even if they express a little awkwardness about being on camera. E-mail the video to the church's tech person (staff or volunteer), so it can quickly be shown through the media in the worship space. The impact on the congregation is incredible! And it is teaching the church not only to use the word *recommend* but also the power of recommendation. Believe me: when the Jenkinses see the affirming video and understand how their simple gesture might change someone's life, they are eager to get out there and recommend the church even more!

This simple technique costs nothing, is easy to do, and is effective. It's not a high-quality production that requires time and dollars, and it doesn't have to be. It's not scripted; it's natural. And it looks like the videos people share all the time from their cell phones—the message and the medium connect.

So when you hear hallway conversation and learn from someone, "I first came here because Sue recommended the support group for people going through divorce," go to that person and ask him or her to tell that story again while you record it on your cell phone to inspire others in the worship service. Most of the time that person will say, "Sure! I'd be happy to do that."

This way you don't have to badger people at the conclusion of the worship service to get out there and recommend the church. Rather, you regularly and consistently show trustimonials. The concept will begin to sink in and become part of the DNA of the church.

Don't be restricted to just Sunday morning screens in worship. Use these trustimonials (even if they are repeats) to start leadership meetings, Sunday school classes, and small groups. Get them on your website and YouTube. Send them out in e-mail blasts to your leaders when you are announcing meetings, so that the leadership begins to see their meeting is not only about an agenda but also about changing lives.

Your job as the leader is to be strategic in deploying the message throughout the congregation. When you do this, you don't have to worry about ministering by yourself. Others will be elevated, lifted, and motivated to become the worker bees. Cast the vision and get it to where it is supposed to be when it is supposed to be.

There are parts of most every congregation still dependent upon print media, so make sure trustimonials (with pictures) are consistently on the pages of your print material.

Second: The pulpit. Preach a sermon or series of sermons on the scriptures highlighted in this chapter. In preparation, be proactive and intentionally engage your congregation's help to develop the sermons. This in itself is a great technique to help your sermons connect more with the congregation. Ask them via e-mail or social media to share personal stories related to the series. For example, if your series is on dating and marriage, ask people to share their "first date" stories, or how they first met. You will receive some fabulous stories! And people will be interested to see if and when their story (or the story of someone they know) might be used.

Build on this strategy by e-mailing (supported by your website, blog, etc.) every member and attender something like this: "Hey, I'm interested in finding out what people in the church really connect with in terms of our ministries, programs, and events. If you have time, please reply to the following quick question: What ministries, programs, or events would you recommend to:

- a new neighbor, or someone you've just met or are just getting to know (perhaps through a social gathering, sporting event, etc.)?

- a family member?

- a friend?

- a coworker?

Now, include some of these stories of recommendation in your message, and also on your website. It's okay to include in the message some instruction on recommending (even using the Stages of Recommendation chart), and to acknowledge that although some folks find it awkward to invite, anyone can recommend!

Who knows? Maybe that seed of recommendation will drop into fertile soil and produce a new follower of Jesus, a person newly active in church and on fire to make a difference in the world, a new friend in the faith.

Third: Reinforce recommendation as often as possible. Do so in meetings, events, worship, Sunday school classes, and so on. Publicly brag on people whose names come up in a recommendation story; send each a personal, handwritten thank-you note for being an influencer in another person's decision to attend church!

The result may look something like this: when John and Theresa Philips visited Faithway Church, meeting in a school auditorium, they had a good experience but concluded the church wasn't for them. The music was too loud, and the service too casual. There were little children everywhere, and the crowd was too young. They quickly decided they would not be returning.

So when they met their new neighbors who had just moved in, do you suppose they invited them to attend Faithway Church with them? No. But they did recommend the church to them! Why? Because the neighbors were a young couple with two children, looking for a church. They had been part of a new church start-up in Michigan and loved it. The Philipses couldn't help but notice that Faithway Church might be a great fit for their new neighbors, so they recommended they try it, which the young family did.

When the pastor wisely captured that story on video and showed it on Sunday morning, she shared an inspirational trustimonial. And she taught the congregation that their recommendations bear fruit! This continued to create and reinforce a strong culture of recommendation within the church.

One reason that recommendation carries so much power is that we occasionally have a situation come up in which we recommend something we don't necessarily like to someone else! This happens because people make assessments about the needs of others and may well recommend your church because they believe it can meet someone else's needs, if not their own.

In the language of the Participant Pyramid (the three R's), the person you've *reached* for the first time doesn't have to *return*, and he or she may still *recommend* your church! That's another reason why recommendation is the easiest, most doable form of evangelism.

When you give people tools they find too hard to use, you just weigh down their toolbox. The advantage of recommendation is that it is a tool that is easy to use, effective, and tends to reinforce itself in a positive manner.

Remember that with the three R's, exponential, fast growth comes from recommending. The next chapter discusses why churches that show accelerated and/or exponential growth do so because they are shifting up to the next gear, closing the consumer/producer gap. The quickest way to close that gap is to get people to recommend the church to someone else. They will be exercising the simplest, most basic way to help produce the ministry of the church, assuming we consider evangelism to be producing the ministry.

Jesus sure taught that it was! The movement from consumer to producer is the movement of a person growing in faith and becoming a disciple—a follower of Jesus. It doesn't really help to grow a church if you are not growing people in their faith, shaping their hearts to have the desire to answer Christ's call to "follow me." But following quickly goes beyond a passive understanding of learning, absorbing, or consuming Jesus' teachings, attitude, and spirit. Jesus himself set the model that to be a disciple is to become a producer.

Jesus said, "Follow me . . . and I will send you out to fish for people" (Matthew 4:19 NIV). Very few times in scripture was Jesus so clear in his expectation of what it means to be a follower. If we're not fishing, then we are not following! Follow me, and I'll make you fishers. Then notice the next line: "At once they left their nets" (v. 20). Talk about the fast track from following to fishing! Jesus wasn't content that people just follow him; he insisted they do something. Moving from a consumer to a producer of the ministry of Christ and your church—that's what it means to be a disciple.

Being a producer is being a fisher. The first and easiest way to fish is to recommend. I (Jim) am a fisherman. When I go to a new lake in a new state, very few fishers just invite me to join them in their boat to fish with them. But almost all will recommend the right lure to use ("what they are biting on"), or the right depth to fish, or the best technique to follow. Most will even point the way to the right place in the lake "where they are hittin' today."

Fishers love to help other fishers catch fish! And one of the best ways to fish for new people is to recommend your church to them, based on what the church has done for you. Or to paraphrase what Jesus said in another context, "Go and tell John what you see and hear. The lame walk and the blind see . . ." (Matthew 11:4-5). Recommending is effective when we tell others what we have personally experienced in the life of the church, how our lives have been impacted and changed by God's grace through Jesus, and what a blessing it is to be part of a caring community of faith.

When people come for the first time, they typically are consumers of what the church has to provide. One of the quickest, easiest, and most fulfilling ways to move them into becoming producers of the church's ministry is to get them simply to recommend the church to others — to get them to "leave their nets at once" and start fishing for new people for the kingdom of God. Recommendation is an easy behavior to teach and encourage, and people will often do it before their second visit!

Follow. Fish. Fast. That will accelerate your church's growth!

Sometimes nothing short of a personal invitation will get another person to experience what you have experienced. There are times when it does take a personal invitation to get somebody over the hump. Perhaps that person is a friend, coworker, or family member. He or she hints of a desire to go to church but can't get up the courage or take the initiative to go. Your personal invitation may be the perfect motivator for that person to come. By all means do it! That's the best fishing! Where inviting is appropriate, invite. Where recommending is appropriate, recommend. The idea is to get fishing faster.

But be cautious that you are not asking someone to ride in the Tour de France, or at least in a cycling marathon, when you expect that person to start fishing by inviting someone to church with him or her. Take care that you do not inadvertently exclude that individual from becoming a producer. You want him or her to quickly produce (recommend), even if he or she is not an accomplished enough rider—or fisher—to be adept at inviting!

Consider a Grandfather Mountain kind of message at the end of your Sunday morning bulletin or worship program: "We hope you were blessed by your experience this morning and will tell a friend about it!"

In the next chapter we'll show how to move people from the first, most basic step of recommending—fishing—into other ways of increasing discipleship by moving people beyond being simply a consumer of the church's ministry to becoming a producer.

Discussion Questions

1. What are some innovative ways you could invite someone to visit your church?

2. What are some innovative ways you could recommend that someone visit your church?

3. Can you think of a time when you recommended your church to someone? Discuss how you were able to do this.

Chapter 10

Turning "Consumers" into "Producers"

Bicycling is a big part of the future. It has to be. There's something wrong with a society that drives a car to work out in a gym.
—*Bill Nye*

When we were learning to ride a bike, many of us learned the hard lesson that the bike had to fit. Didn't this happen to you? Once you learned to ride, and saw how easy it was, you were eager to get out there and jump on a bike—any bike. You watched with envy as a friend rode by on her brand-new, sparkling, tricked-out bike, those little plastic streamers coming out of the handlebar, flapping in the wind. And then she let you have a turn! Only problem was—the bike didn't fit. You needed a twenty-four incher, and hers was a twenty-eight incher. Still, you tried. It just didn't work well.

If the seat isn't adjusted to fit the rider, bad things can happen. You can still ride, but it's likely to be wobbly, and you may well fall over when you try to stop. When it comes to your church's ministry, to fit means to be real, authentic, and genuine. We have too many churches that go to seminars put on by megachurches or read books (even this book) and then try to make that big, successful church's or that book's techniques fit them. They are twenty-four inchers trying to ride a twenty-eight incher. Even if they are able to ride, there are likely to be wobbles and falls—bruised relationships and scrapes on the soft skin of young Christians. They may still move forward, but there are too many times tipping over trying to figure out this whole church thing.

We are moving into the discussion about moving your people beyond consumers and helping them to become producers. This is a delicate discussion because your efforts will have to fit you and your church. You may see some reasons to change some of the ways you are approaching first-time guests, but what we have to share here comes from our experience. For that reason, we want to stress how important it is that you tweak and modify what we have to share in a way that is genuine and authentic for you and your church. You may have to adjust the seat so it fits! Do it. Our goal here is to give you the tools, not to tell you exactly how it should be done.

This section is about shifting gears to accelerate growth, which includes churches learning to close the consumer/producer gap . . . faster! In a new church plant, virtually everyone is a "producer" doing something to "make it happen." It may be setting up chairs, distributing water bottles at the park, delivering food to the homeless shelter, or becoming part of the band. But, as churches age, they gradually drift into more of a "consumer" mentality that slows growth. Often people attend a church for the first time as consumers of what the church has to offer. This is fine, but the faster the church is able to turn those consumers into "producers" of the church's ministry, the more accerlerated the growth becomes.

Guests return for two reasons: One reason is that they liked it!

130

They had a good experience or, in the nomenclature of the business world, enjoyed a good product. This first reason is a must for your church to grow. It generates growth. The second reason people return is that they get involved. This is what accelerates growth. As we discussed earlier, the relationships and friendships that develop when people are "doing things together" foster the "connections" that lead to growth. The faster you can get a first-time attender (a consumer) to become involved (a producer), the faster you will grow.

In Matthew 16:3, Jesus criticized religious leaders for their lack of awareness in "interpret[ing] the signs of the times" (NIV). Perhaps today we have an equally hard time reading the signs of the times in our changing world. Mainline churches still tend to operate under the strategy that if we produce the best possible product, people will come to consume it instead of going down the street to another church. This strategy, and the assumptions behind it, may not actually match reality. The target audience has changed—most people won't give up two hours on a Sunday morning simply to consume! Leverage the desire by most people today to want to produce! And these are the kind of people necessary to create exponential growth in a church.

Over five hundred thousand home-based businesses start every month in America. While there is certainly a strong thread of consumerism rampant in America, people in our culture are more geared to produce than most of us realize. In the church, the faster we can turn a consumer into a producer, the faster we'll grow. How long does it take in your church? Days? Weeks? Months? Years? This generation wants to make a difference, and one underlying question guests have is how they can make a difference through the life of your church. If there are too many barriers, if it takes too long to be a producer, they will divert their attention elsewhere.

Being a consumer is not necessarily bad. Our national economy is dependent upon people consuming various products and services.

In fact, people's ability to survive and live is a function of consuming food, water, and social stimulation. But the economy truly thrives when a significant number of consumers turn into producers of those various products and services—and new ones! This entrepreneurial spirit drives societies forward because it is impossible for a producer to produce without also consuming the raw products needed for production.

The same dynamic operates within a church. We all have seasons in our lives when we need to consume the gospel the church offers; there are times when we need to be ministered to and served and nourished and strengthened spiritually in any number of ways. That is why the church exists. But it cannot continue to exist unless a significant number of consumers turn into producers! And producers will shrivel up and waste away—spiritually and otherwise—if they do not continue to consume the life-giving nourishment of the gospel.

When we talk about consumers and producers, we are not talking about them in mutually exclusive terms—as an *either/or*. It is a matter of *both/and*, so our conversation has the underlying foundation that both are good and that each is dependent upon the other. We are talking about the intentional movement of turning a consumer into a producer of the church's ministry, for the specific purpose of growing the church.

To consume is not bad. But if too many people in a church remain consumers only, that is bad; the church cannot sustain itself. Sustainability and viability are dependent upon getting consumers to realize that they must also be producers and be equipped to do so—so that others can be impacted by the same power of the gospel that impacted them. Unfortunately, in too many churches, too many people have become content with being consumers, and we are seeing the growth of the church slip into decline, the impact in the world being stifled. Let's talk about how we can close the consumer/producer gap in your church.

132

A good product doesn't really accelerate growth; it solidifies it. People can be returning to our church on a regular basis, and if we are not careful, we inadvertently train them to be happy, satisfied consumers of our Sunday morning product. And that is where they'll stay.

Out of a sense of decline and desperation, most mainline churches are making a conscientious effort to become more outwardly focused by changing many things about their facility, messaging, and ministry. But if the culture of the church is still inwardly focused, changing all the things in the world won't make much difference. It starts with changing the culture, which travels on words. We often see this when a church asks us to assess their first-time visitor letter. Usually this is a form letter, sent out by snail mail or e-mail if the church is fortunate enough to get contact information from the guest. Typically, the letter will be friendly in style, with the pastor's signature, and read something like this:

Dear _____,

We are so glad you joined us in worship last Sunday! Here at Christ Church we have the joy of experiencing inspiring music, uplifting messages, and great fellowship every week! I hope you sensed the warmth and friendship of our church and will come again soon.

As you can see, we have many outstanding programs for children, youth, and adults—something to meet your needs no matter where you are in your faith journey.

If you have any questions, or if we can help you in any way, please don't hesitate to contact us. I look forward to getting better acquainted in the days ahead.

In Christ's name,

_____

This truly is a warm and friendly letter that is intended to be nice and welcoming. It is. But let's consider some ways it could be made stronger and avoid unwittingly training the first-time guest to become a consumer right from the start. The more we train our participants to be consumers, the harder it is to retrain and motivate them to become producers. This kind of letter in and of itself is not a problem. The problem is that it more than likely reflects the underlying culture of the church, one that is more consumer- than producer-oriented.

Consider the impact of crafting the letter in a way that says that the intention of the church is to passionately introduce a first-time guest to opportunities not only to be blessed, but also to be a blessing to others through meaningful service.

Dear _____,

Thank you for being in worship at Christ Church last week! We know it's a big step to get up on Sunday morning and go to a new church for the first time; thanks again!

I hope your presence indicates you have a passion for making a difference in the community and in the world. Then again, maybe you have something going on in your life and you are looking for answers, or you may have been in worship for some other reason altogether. Whatever the reason, we hope that you benefitted from the effort you made to be here.

Within the next few days you'll be contacted about ways you can put your passion, talents, and skills to work for the glory of God, if you have that interest at this point in your life. You'll hear about ways that can make a lasting impact and match who you are and where you are in your spiritual journey.

I hope you enjoyed your experience and will tell a friend about it. If you have any questions, please don't hesitate to text or call me at _____.

Thanks again,

_____

It's only fair to note that if you know the first-time guest is a member's family member from out of town, or not really a prospect to become an active participant in your church's life, then the first letter would probably be the better letter to send.

However, if you know the guest is truly a potential participant (perhaps by contact information such as address or other qualifying information), then the second letter is probably the better letter to send. It is to your advantage to have multiple targeted letters ready to send to various first-time guests! You want the letter (and other ways you follow up with guests) to fit your church and your personality. Just make sure your responses—tweaked to your style—are modeled along the key components of hospitality: intentionality, relationship, interaction, engagement, and connection.

But did you notice the differences in the two letters? Let's look closer at the second letter: Did you notice that it is intentionally crafted to immediately start the journey of turning a first-time guest into a producer? The first paragraph gushes thanks, and clearly sends the message the letter is about *them*, not *us*. The second paragraph leads with the producer nudge and then acknowledges in a softer way that whatever the reason they attended, you hope *they* benefited! And then it gives advance notice of an intentional effort to get them involved in some serving way so they can be prepared. They may simply choose not to pick up the phone if they see the church's number on the caller ID, or they may start to think of questions they may want to ask when they are called. The last paragraph of the letter is simply personal and friendly, but with no expectations (which can often seem to an unchurched person like guilting).

Now look closer at the first letter, which is the more typical example of a first time visitor letter. While the church probably wouldn't think so, the receiver of the letter might well perceive that the letter is really about the church, not the guest—not *them* but *us*! The guest "joined us." And who benefited? The pastor and the church—the guest's visit made them "so glad"! It's wonderful that the guest's action made the church glad, but it really is supposed to be the other way around. This mixed-up message isn't intentional, and doesn't mean the church leadership isn't thoughtful and considerate. It just happens as churches slip into routines. Sometimes, the perspective of an outsider can be helpful to see what those in the trenches simply overlook and don't even consider.

My (Jim's) guess is that the first line of that letter was crafted simply to assure guests that they could count on high-quality music, messages, and hospitality every week. It was a message about consistency and quality. This is not a bad thing, but if we're not careful, this unnecessary tactic can sometimes lead an unchurched, first-time guest to draw a different conclusion than the church intended. Believe me: if first-time guests haven't already checked out your website, they certainly will if they think they may be interested in what the church has to offer.

Notice the messaging: *You* come join *us*. Consume *our* friendliness, *our* music, *our* message, *our* programming. Again, this is unintentional, but the language is distancing, drawing an unneeded distinction between us and them. Consequently, it doesn't readily connect with the receiver like the church probably thinks it does.

What else did you notice? Can you see how both letters can be helpful, depending upon what your intent and strategy might be?

We have been talking about the church's response to a first-time guest. In many churches, before guests receive a follow-up e-mail or letter, someone in the church has already contacted the guest. Follow-up may be via text message or e-mail, or perhaps someone on some team has dropped off a mug or loaf of bread to the guest's home.

You may want to consider a pre-visit contact with guests. It is generally acknowledged that before a guest attends the church, he or she will have visited your website; at least that seems to be the growing trend in the United States. So right there on the church's website or Facebook page, set the culture as that of making producers. In Dallas, the Village Church—one of the fastest-growing churches in America—says clearly on their website: "While we minister to each other, our deepest desire is to equip and train our church body to bring the gospel to their families, community, and world." This church is communicating in short that they want to prepare people to become producers of their ministry, which is defined as sharing the gospel.

To get first-time guests to return, you must have a good product, and you must get them involved quickly to move them beyond being just a consumer to becoming a producer. What accelerates growth is closing this gap quickly. In fast-growing churches the process begins even before the guest arrives and is intentionally continued immediately following the guest's first visit.

When we talk about getting people involved, we don't mean going into über-attack mode to sign them up for some necessary job or task that you are having trouble filling from your regular attenders. Newcomers can quickly sense they are fresh meat to a struggling church.

You may be really fortunate: Your first-time guest may have been an influential leader at Willow Creek Community Church outside of Chicago, Illinois, or Resurrection, in Leawood, Kansas, before moving to your area! He or she may be well trained, accustomed to tithing, and equipped and ready to jump into action. But to plan for that is to wait for your fantasy guest! More likely, your guest will not already be an outstanding, veteran church person. This is okay, because it probably means a first-time guest is an unchurched or disconnected person, which is precisely your target audience!

Many, if not most, of your first-time guests will be folks who haven't yet been through a spiritual gifts inventory class; they will have little knowledge of or appreciation for all the myriad functions, tasks, and slots that most local churches need to fill to be able to operate effectively. We are not talking about fast-tracking newcomers into these responsibilities. We are talking about creating an environment where they quickly buy into the mission and ministry of *some aspect* of the church and are willing to step into a carefully designed expression of that ministry.

By *carefully designed* we mean a ministry area that is: (1) safe, (2) sensible, (3) short-term, (4) satisfying, and (5) significant.

1. Safe—The context of the ministry doesn't put a brand-new person into a situation that may be awkward, too risky, or too far out of their comfort zone.

2. Sensible—Does it make sense, from the perspective of the generational age and stage of the person you are hoping to involve? Would the person believe the task to be worth doing? Could the person explain its value to a friend?

3. Short term—A good "one and done" hands-on opportunity works best. It may continue or expand, but there is no expectation that it will.

4. Satisfying—This is still a "feel good" generation. When the person reflects on what she or he has done, will that individual be satisfied?

5. Significant—This is the most important characteristic. Will the participant truly feel the or she has made a difference for the cause, or to another person? Does it have kingdom impact, and can it help change the world?

The function of leadership is to clarify and communicate exactly what it is that you would consider a core ministry of your church—to make sure the specific ministry fits into the life of your church and to make sure you have adjusted the seat so a new person can get on and ride. What kind of ministries—following the 5 S's above—can you offer that a first-time guest can quickly get involved with?

Some years ago, during the time when many of our current clergy were being trained and entering into the ministry, the accepted model of involvement looked like this:

Ministry Function within the Church > Hands-On Helping Outside the Church > Inviting

But today, times have changed. And the most successful model is like this:

Recommending > Hands-On Helping Outside Church > Ministry Function within Church

We have to read the signs of the times and adjust our approach to getting people involved. We must close the consumer/producer gap by focusing on moving people beyond consumers to producers. How you do this task must fit your church, but be intentional. The faster you can do it, the faster your church will grow!

Discussion Questions

1. Do you like the idea of "checking in" on Facebook during church? Why or why not?

2. What would you recommend about your church?

3. What would you not recommend about your church?

Endurance: The Lasting Impression of Culture

The bicycle has done more for the emancipation
of women than anything else in the world.
—Susan B. Anthony

"What do you call a bunch of bees together?" The zoo guide's question was intentionally designed to be interactive and engaging.

"A hive!" shouted out nearly all of the kids in his tour group.

"Well, how about a bunch of birds together?" the guide asked, shining a playful smile.

"A flock!" came their resounding reply.

A zoo trip is good anytime, especially for an elementary school class's end-of-the-year field trip. The bus had parked, and out romped twenty-eight students and their parent sponsors. Trip planners had lined up the zoo's friendliest guide. The guide, in turn, arranged for sodas, ice cream, and peanuts for his group, showing great hospitality.

"Oh, very good, indeed!" he said, "Now, here's a harder one: What do you call a bunch of cows together?" He asked it with mock intensity.

"A herd!" The voices almost screamed in unison.

"Now, here's a really hard one," challenged the guide. "What do you call a bunch of vultures together?"

"Uh, vultures," was all the kids could say.

"All right, I'll tell you," snapped the guide. "A bunch of vultures together is called a committee!"

The kids laughed because the word sounded funny. The parents laughed because, well, you know why the grown-ups laughed. The guide's answer rang true for most of them.

"That's right," intoned the guide, "A group of vultures together is called a committee of vultures." The parents laughed again, relating to the irony of it. Then the guide sped on excitedly, as the group meandered in front of the rhino natural habitat exhibit.

"Okay, here's the hardest one: What do you call a group of rhinos together?"

Before they could guess at an answer, the guide continued, "Let me explain some things about rhinos, as a hint. Rhinos are really big, as you can see. They have that ugly horn coming out their snout, and they have tough, tough skin. And even though their legs are short and they stand close to the ground, they can run really fast, sometimes up to thirty-five miles an hour! Well, maybe because they are so big, they rumble more than run, but they still do it fast! The problem is, they have poor vision and can see only about thirty feet in front of them!"

The kids oohed and aahed. Then the guide brought his lesson to an impressive finish—a learning moment for those present. "So since rhinos can run thirty-five miles an hour but can only see thirty feet in front of them, here's what you call a group of rhinos together: a crash of rhinos!"

The parents laughed, which caused the kids to laugh.

Said the guide insightfully, "It's true. A group of rhinos together is a called a crash of rhinos, because if you have a group of rhinos running through the underbrush at thirty-five miles an hour while they can only see thirty feet, then you are heading for a crash!"

This humorous story has circulated among pastors and church staff for some time. It's popular because it's true. If you run faster than your vision, you are heading for a crash. The same can be said for a church or any organization.

We, the authors of this book, are in the United Methodist tribe. We've shared many stories of things we've heard and experienced over the years. Sometimes we wonder if the truth about the rhinos will also be the fate of The United Methodist Church and other denominations. Are we really just rugged old institutions, so loaded up with complicated boards, committees, hierarchies, and structures that we appear to move slowly but in reality rumble along so fast that we outrun our vision?

If we run faster than our vision, we are headed for a crash.

In the preceding section we talked about how to accelerate church growth. But we do not mean you should have speed that exceeds your vision. That will only end up in a crash. What allows the rider to keep riding is not only avoiding crashes, but perhaps more importantly, endurance. Every rider knows that practice, practice, practice develops the stamina that results in endurance—the ability to ride for the long haul.

For our purposes, endurance is the result of the intentional creation of your church's culture, that mystical combination of vision, values, and purpose. Without a good, strong, clear, irresistible culture, your church will either crash or not ride long.

We have shared techniques to help create a culture of hospitality. The 5-10-Link is a simple tool you can use to do so in your setting. It is designed for maximum effectiveness with these goals in mind:

- It must be taught clearly, and at least annually, in worship, Sunday school classes, other groups, and to staff;

- It must be modeled constantly by the senior pastor, staff, and lay leadership;

- It must be practiced consistently by *every member, every Sunday*;

- It must be prioritized convincingly throughout the church as a core value.

The degree to which your church is successful at reaching the above goals will determine in large part the culture of hospitality that will become pivotal to the DNA of your congregation. No church is going to become adept at all four goals all the time, but we can keep trying. It won't happen all at once, but it can happen little by little.

We try to encourage congregations with the timely story found in Exodus 23:20-30, where God leads God's people to the promised land. They hear the assurance that God is sending an angel ahead of them, to direct them, coach them, and protect them. But God acknowledges there are too many obstacles and enemies to overcome, and even though God *can* do it, God *won't* do it too quickly. Realistically, the people just wouldn't be ready and the situation wouldn't be right!

But in verse 30 we see clearly: *"Little by little I will drive them out before you, until you have increased enough to take possession of the land"* (NIV).

The hospitality we're talking about is a divine thing. Don't expect it to happen all at once. Your church wouldn't even be ready for it. But little by little, following God's guidance and good preparation, your church can move into the promised land of a culture of hospitality.

So let's summarize these simple, doable prerequisites:

- Teaching the 5-10-Link: Doing so is fun and engaging, and provides a high-energy experience in worship each and every time it is taught. If creating a culture of hospitality is indeed a high priority, then it is not sufficient to teach it at a Wednesday night meeting of the hospitality team. Rather, on a designated Sunday each year (or maybe even twice a year), it must be the theme of morning worship.

- Modeling the 5-10-Link by the pastor(s), staff, and lay leadership: This quickly becomes an affirming, positive set of behaviors that become second nature and natural.

- Having members consistently practice the 5-10-Link: Obviously not everyone is going to buy into the concept—some because of stubbornness, and others simply because it is so different from their wiring that they can't cross over into a realm outside their comfort zone. But the closer we can get to *every member* practicing it *every Sunday*, the more it will become the culture of the church.

- Prioritizing hospitality as a high value in the church: When we do this, we will give appropriate time to it, direct funds toward it, and be intentional about it.

Our objective in this book has been to convince readers that creating a culture of hospitality is as easy as riding a bike! You don't have to be riding uphill, into the wind all the time. You can find your pace and ride the winds of your local church culture and in denominational hierarchies. Balance and momentum are what keep your bike from falling over. But there is one last key ingredient to moving forward. We've saved it for this epilogue. Endurance. Endurance is what keeps the rider riding for the long haul. For the church, organizational culture leads to endurance. Your culture—the culture you want to embed in the life of your church—is what will translate your effort into energy and endurance!

Culture is often introduced as a new way of doing things in a given arena that may seem strange and weird to many people, some of whom may be successful veterans or even experts in that arena. In our fast-changing world, the shock of newness gradually leads to the ability to overcome resistance, while the new way of doing things yields incredible results. Almost amazingly, the new paradigm becomes the accepted way of doing things (like Google changing the workplace, or Southwest Airlines having fun!). Then it becomes the expected way of doing things. Your culture of hospitality will become an expected behavior in the church. On those rare days when it is not up to par, people will sense it and miss it!

Remember that a culture of hospitality is a subset of the larger culture in the church. It must match or be consistent with the dominant culture of the church. So as leaders, pastors must become better at creating intentional culture for their church.

A good, healthy culture is not designed to get an organization to connect better to its customer base or mission field. But the result is that the customer base or mission field will want to connect! Bad, unhealthy culture causes people to run, or at best not to engage.

Remember those three short phrases that capture the culture of Southwest Airlines: "Warrior Spirit," "Servant's Heart," and "Fun-LUVing Attitude." Former CEO Herb Kelleher intentionally developed them, and then taught them to his key associates and executive staff, and then taught them to the next tier of employees, and on and on until they were embedded throughout the culture. Now, not only does everyone in the organization know these phrases, but they also practice them! Culture leaks. It takes intentional effort to keep filling up the organization with the culture. Most Southwest customers don't know those culture words, but they feel the impact of that culture daily. Pastors—your top priority as a leader is to create and maintain the culture of the church. Start with hospitality, which is the easiest part of church culture to create, and you and others will see a lasting impression.

Consider this summary of the impact of bicycling in America:

> The bicycle was . . . a practical investment for the working man as transportation, and gave him a much greater flexibility for leisure. Ladies, heretofore consigned to riding the heavy adult-size tricycles that were only practical for taking a turn around the park, now could ride a much more versatile machine and still keep their legs covered with long skirts. The bicycle craze killed the bustle and the corset, instituted "common-sense dressing" for women and increased their mobility considerably. In 1896, Susan B. Anthony said that "the bicycle has done more for the emancipation of women than anything else in the world."
>
> Bicycling was so popular in the 1880s and 1890s that cyclists formed the League of American Wheelmen (still in existence and now called the League of American Bicyclists). The League lobbied for better roads, literally paving the road for the automobile. ("A Quick History of Bicycles," Pedaling History Bicycle Museum, http://www.pedalinghistory.com/PHhistory.html)

What is the lasting impression of culture? We started this book by showing that bicycle riding is a learned skill. Even though most of us had help, there were parts of the learning process we had to do on our own. Those who were helping us had to let us go, so we could balance and pedal by ourselves. And yet once we could do this, we could enjoy the company of other riders. Bicycling is typically a shared behavior. Once we learned to ride, we did so with friends, and riding became a part of our lives in ways that have impacted us since. On many college campuses and even in some cities, like New York, bike sharing is now part of the culture. The college, or the city, provides bikes that a student, or resident, can ride from one place to another, and can leave at that location. Another person then picks up the bike and rides it somewhere else. On and on it goes. A skill each person learned years ago is now a shared behavior as part of the culture.

Creating an enduring culture of hospitality goes well beyond being warm and friendly and polite at church. It can and should go deeper. Consider Jesus' words in Matthew 25:35-36: "I was hungry and you gave me food, I was thirsty and you gave me something to drink, I was a stranger and you welcomed me, I was naked and you gave me clothing, I was sick and you took care of me, I was in prison and you visited me" (NRSV). These words are often argued from a theological or even national policy perspective, but for Jesus maybe those verses were first and foremost a matter of hospitality. Perhaps creating a culture of hospitality in our churches might influence the hospitality we show in the world to those we do not yet know or understand all that well.

When hospitality becomes a shared behavior in your church, you've created a culture of hospitality. So hop on and clip in—start riding today!

You should ride your bike for twenty minutes a day, unless you're too busy; then you should ride for an hour.
—Zen adage, adapted for bicyclers
(Always Wear a Helmet When Riding)

Discussion Questions

1. Did you receive a "first-time visitor" letter? If so, what were your feelings about it? If not, did you expect one?

2. How would you describe the culture of your church?

3. What are some elements of your church's culture you are excited about? What are some you are concerned about?

4. What is one of the main tools you learned from this book that you want to implement in your own church?

5. Read Matthew 25:35-45. What are some implications of Jesus' words when it comes to creating a culture of hospitality in your church?

Made in the USA
San Bernardino, CA
03 August 2017